Student Guide

>>> essential reading

for life at university

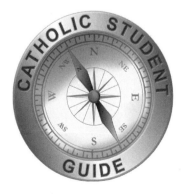

Publisher's Note

The Catholic Student Guide has been produced as an independent initiative by Family Publications, under the direction of the editor, Peter Kahn. The Guide is not associated with any of the organisations or institutions mentioned in this Guide, nor does it give any of them special endorsement. We have tried as far as possible to create a guide with a broad appeal, which adheres to the teaching of the Catholic Church. While every effort has been made to obtain accurate information from the chaplaincies and organisations featured in Part II, its accuracy is entirely dependent upon the information submitted by them, and may be subject to change. We welcome your comments, corrections or additional material for inclusion in future editions, which can be sent to catholicstudent@hotmail.com or to the editor, c/o the publishers at the address below. New editions will normally appear biannually. Selected additional materials may be posted on the associated website, www.catholicstudent.net.

This Guide will be made available in alternative formats. Please contact Catholic Blind Services, PO Box 10333, Birmingham B13 8XX. Tel: 07973 908274.

Contents

Editors' Acknowledgements

We are grateful to Archbishop Vincent Nichols for his encouragement and for kindly providing the Foreword, and to Cardinal Cormac Murphy O'Connor and Archbishop Mario Conti for their support for the project.

We would also like to thank all the benefactors for their generous financial contributions towards this project, which have enabled the Guide to be made available at a price substantially below cost.

A large number of people have helped to create this Guide: the authors of the chapters; the students and recent graduates who shared their experiences; and all those who lent us photographs or supplied information for the listings in the second part. We are grateful to all of these individuals for their contribution to the Guide.

While responsibility for the content rests with the editors, we are particularly grateful to Fr Peter Conley, to the numerous reviewers, and to the Conference of Catholic Chaplains in Higher Education, whose comments have helped to shape the final version.

Producing a Guide on this scale involves a range tasks, and thanks are also due to Nick Simm for data entry, Alison Kahn for contacting organisations, and all of the staff at Family Publications.

On a personal note, Peter would like to thank his own family for their support in what was a seemingly endless task. So, thank you Alison, David and Joachim.

Foreword

In 1994 Pope John Paul published a book. Popes usually issue Encyclical Letters and other formal documents. But this was a book. It is called *Crossing the Threshold of Hope*.

In fact the book is made up of a series of answers he had written, in his spare time, to a set of questions he had received from a journalist. They had been sent to him in the hope of arranging a major interview with the Holy Father. That had proved to be impossible. But the written answers arrived instead.

In *Crossing the Threshold of Hope* the Pope wrote about young people. The question he had been given was "Is there really hope in young people?" In his answer he spoke about the experiences of his own youth and went on to say:

"The experiences of teachers and pastors confirm, today no less than yesterday, the idealism present in young people, even if nowadays it perhaps tends to be expressed mostly in the form of criticism, whereas before it would have translated more simply into duty."

The Pope then adds:

"What is youth? It is not only a period of life that corresponds to a certain number of years, it is also a time given by Providence to every person and given as a responsibility. During that time the young person searches, like the young man in the Gospel, for answers to basic questions; he searches not only for the meaning of life, but also for a concrete way to go about living life. This is the most fundamental characteristic of youth." (pp. 120–121)

With these two points in mind, I welcome the publication of this *Catholic Student Guide*. I think it corresponds well to the insights of Pope John Paul: that young people have within themselves great idealism, and that the years of youth are a search for a personal way of life.

I am sure that many young people, setting out from their school years, will find this guide helpful. I thank those who have worked hard to put it together and to make it available.

We are right to have high hopes of young people today.

+Vincent Nichols
Archbishop of Birmingham
8 August 2003

About the editors

Dr Peter Kahn, Editor, is an educational developer at the University of Manchester, where he works with lecturers to help improve teaching across the university. He has been an active member of the Catholic community in five universities or university colleges over a period of 17 years, and is a member of a parish-based community that is largely made up of young Catholics.

Fr Jeremy Fairhead, Consulting Editor, is Catholic chaplain to Oxford University, and was previously Catholic chaplain to the Universities of London for six years. He has a special interest in catechetics.

About the contributors

Susan Holloway is an 18-year-old who has recently left school. She is currently doing a gap year in Granada, Spain, where she is teaching English in a Catholic School. Susan studied History, English and French for 'A' Level and is going to study History at Sheffield University.

Fiorella Sultana De Maria studied English Literature at New Hall College, Cambridge, followed by an MPhil in Medieval and Renaissance Literature at Darwin College, Cambridge, which she completed last year. She is currently working at the Society for the Protection of Unborn Children, and is a columnist for the *Catholic Herald*. Her interests include the Middle East, human rights, writing, reading and music.

Julie and Cyrus Olsen are graduates of the universities of Washington in Seattle, and Oxford (Cyrus), and San Francisco and Notre Dame Graduate School of Christendom College in Alexandria, VA (Julie). Julie teaches RE at a Catholic girls' school in Oxford. Cyrus is a DPhil candidate at the University of Oxford. They were married in 2002.

Fr Joseph Evans studied French and Portuguese at King's College, London, and worked as a journalist and youth worker before his ordination as a priest in 2001. He is now full-time chaplain to Netherhall House, a university hall of residence for students in London.

Damien Morley is currently teaching English in France as part of a French degree at King's College London. He has been involved with Youth 2000 for six years, initially as a participant and later as an organiser. His claim to fame is that he has been selected for the French national cricket team!

Terrenia Brosnan is a third-year medical student at North Staffordshire City General Hospital. She has lived in both Manchester and Cambridge as a student and enjoys singing, acting, getting involved in recycling programmes, peace vigils, pro-life work and prayer groups, all while pretending to study hard! Youth 2000 has also been a great source of friendship and encouragement for her over the last four years.

WHAT'S IT ALL ABOUT?
Peter Kahn

Welcome to the Catholic Student Guide

What is it all about? – The Guide offers a Catholic perspective on student life and access to opportunities offered by a range of organisations. If you are thinking of going to university or are already there, then this Guide has plenty for you. Parents, teachers, chaplains and others too will find much here to share with students.

The Guide presumes that you have some interest in the Catholic faith. Perhaps, however, you have seriously questioned the relevance of faith to your life. University provides a time for you to reassess things – so take advantage of the opportunity. Why not dip into a chapter in the first part of the Guide or get in touch with one of the organisations that are listed in the second part?

You may, instead, be convinced about your faith but reluctant to let anyone else know. Take a look at what Alice says on the next page about her own reticence in letting anyone know she was a Catholic when she first went to university. If you are a little more open, you also may find that your faith is worth sharing with others. Meanwhile, for Catholics who are confident about their faith, the reality is that you will need support on your spiritual journey, especially if going to university coincides with a move away from home, or even overseas.

Insight into student life . . .

The first part consists of seven chapters that each look at a different aspect of student life. The chapters also include one or two views from students or recent graduates, whose experiences offer insight into what life is like if you want to live out your faith at university.

For prospective students, there is the decision as to where to go for university – hence the first chapter. Fr Jeremy explores the issues involved in making this choice. You may, of course, choose to take a gap year at some point; the second chapter considers the possibilities, and is written by someone who was taking a gap year even while writing the chapter – Susan Holloway. The next chapter is on accommodation, something that prospective students will need to think about even before they begin their studies, but which is also relevant for every student. A recent graduate, Fiorella, reviews the options on where to live.

University life is, of course, about study. Fr Joe considers why it is worth investing yourself in your studies. We then go on to look at lifestyle issues, with Julie and Cyrus taking a look at the social world at university. In the next chapter, two students, Terrenia and Damien, focus on our relationship with God and how we can develop it. They are convinced that we need God's help if we are to find fulfilment. The Guide finally covers life after university. Even if this seems a world away, the last chapter still has something to say to you now.

...and plenty of information

The second part lists a wide range of organisations that have something to offer Catholic students. First of all, there are details on what is available near to universities, listed on a regional basis. Each university or college has a Catholic chaplain, and the chaplaincy is very much the centre of Catholic life in most universities. E-mail the chaplain so that you can find out what is going on, or pop into the chaplaincy – you are sure to receive a warm welcome. There is also a range of other groups which offer you a home while at university; why not get in touch and see what they have to offer? Finally, in these regional listings, there are details of any accommodation that is organised on a Catholic basis, and details of opportunities to help those in need.

STUDENT VIEW: Foiled by a direct question

I had decided before I went to university that I wouldn't let anyone know I was a Catholic too quickly. I realised that for the first time in my life, I could portray to people exactly what I wanted to say about myself – nobody knew me, who I was or where I'd come from. I didn't want people to judge me or decide what they thought about me just because I was a Christian.

God, however, obviously had other plans. The moment I met my first housemate, she asked the question "Are you at all religious?" Faced with such a direct question, I felt I couldn't lie, and blurted out that I was.

As it turned out, I needn't in fact have worried too much about being open about my faith. I soon found that my friends, even those from no faith background, were not only interested in what I believed, but also respectful of the way I chose to live my life. But there were many times when one or other of my housemates would pull me up, with questions like "Should you really be doing that if you're a Christian?"

And if I was representing the Christian Faith to my non-Christian friends, I also soon found out that I was the face of the Catholic Church to my Protestant friends. This reality of a divided Church hit me right in my first week at university, when I was told by an Evangelical friend that I clearly wasn't a Christian if I was a Catholic!

All of these challenges to my faith made me realise how little I knew about it. When people asked me about my beliefs, I could never give them an answer – highlighting a real lack of knowledge about what I was saying to people when I called myself a Catholic! I soon found myself questioning and discovering what Catholics believe. And for the first time I also found myself really beginning to live out what I believe.

Alice Hall, recent graduate from University of Kent at Canterbury

The listings then cover national organisations that offer services or opportunities for Catholic students. You can find out about organisations that support students with disabilities, about the new movements and communities, and a wide range of other groups. There are also listings for Catholic institutions that offer higher education courses, and entries for organisations that offer gap years or advice and information on taking a gap year. Last of all, we include details of websites that will be of interest, particularly for resources about your faith. All of these listings will assist you in tracking down support to live out your Catholic faith at university. You will also find any corrections to these listings, as well as additional entries, on our companion website: www.catholicstudent.net

A Catholic view

The Guide makes no apology for taking the Catholic faith seriously. *The Catechism of the Catholic Church,* with its summary of Catholic teaching, provides a particular reference point, as do the writings and sermons of Pope John Paul II and other important figures. Ideas are also taken from the Bible, since as Catholics we believe that God speaks to us there. The Guide further stresses the importance of friendships with other Catholics. My own involvement in several Catholic groups has convinced me that young Catholics need to support each other in whatever ways they can. Indeed, this conviction was part of the inspiration behind the Guide.

Freedom !

What then is life at university all about? Of course it involves study, too much debt and in many cases whatever employment can be had; but for many students it's also about unrestricted freedom – to have a good time. The Guide, however, offers you a fresh take on freedom – true freedom is the opportunity to love and serve others and to love and serve God. In the current student climate this really is a *radical* approach – yet it is the one that brings true fulfilment in life. Enjoy the Guide!

MAKING CHOICES
Fr Jeremy Fairhead

The choice of where to go for higher education is one of the most important choices we make in our lives. It shapes us for the future in ways that we cannot imagine. University is more than just a chance to learn about a subject or acquire academic skills; it is an opportunity to discover yourself. For many, their time at university is their first experience of living away from home and being their own person – even to the extent of re-creating themselves.

This, then, is an important decision and one which should not be taken lightly; to paraphrase St Paul, we cannot expect good decisions to arise simply on the spur of the moment, without any concern to try and find out what is right (cf. *Romans* 12:2). As Christians, we believe that God has given us the gift of freedom; we have the freedom to make our own choices, good and bad, but we also have the responsibility to make them after adequate thought.

Choosing which university to go to, however, is far from easy. A student at my own chaplaincy put it this way: "Hundreds of those glossy prospectuses and the pressures to discern my career path – it was all information overload and far too stressful." So it is worth taking a look at some of the factors you will need to take into consideration: subject; ability; location; finance; direction after graduation; and finally your faith. Thinking about each of these issues will help you to find a way through the mass of information.

Now, later, or never?

First of all, though, you will have to think quite carefully as to whether this is the right time for you to study at University. The fact that your friends are embarking upon higher education is not a good enough reason in itself for you to do so as well. It may be worth waiting for a time – to take advantage of other opportunities and to gear yourself up for this next step. For many, a gap year is an invaluable experience which makes their time at university more fruitful; and more people than you might think only go to university later on, in their twenties. So you should bear in mind that you are under no obligation to follow your friends onto the teenage-student bandwagon.

Be Inspired

By the time you begin to take your final exams at school, however, it should be clear where both your strengths and interests lie. Most people have the option of choosing one or two subjects around different academic traditions: the arts and humanities, science and, increasingly, vocational subjects. You may find yourself naturally tending towards a subject you are good at or which you think will give you the best career opportunities. These are important issues, but a subject should also *inspire* you. You are going to spend three, four, or maybe more years reading, writing and speaking about it. You need to have more than a mercenary interest or simple natural talent if you are going to both enjoy your studies and take anything of long-term value away from your degree.

It is also important to note that it is not just a question of choosing a subject that you like and a university you feel comfortable with – the two cannot be separated in your deliberations. Courses vary considerably from place to place, both in terms of the topics studied and in the way that they are studied. For instance, some history degrees offer no medieval papers, while other courses insist that you do at least one. Courses also place different emphases on the balance between examinations and coursework, and even on the amount of student group work. All of these factors can profoundly influence your enjoyment of the course and your level of achievement, and are important considerations too often overlooked.

Town or Campus?

A further issue you need to consider is the physical environment of the universities at which you are looking. Not everyone is suited to all the styles on offer, most prominent of which are the campus or town environments. A campus university at-

tempts to offer a cohesive community and a clear sense of belonging and identity, but at the same time you may find yourself bewildered and lost in a large concrete city where anonymity seems to be the watchword.

The town environment is another option, but again you have to be careful because the benefits of being more integrated within a "normal" urban community are not always so clear, especially when the different parts of the university are sprawled out over several sites across town, forcing you to travel sometimes long distances. Each style has its own strengths and weaknesses which are more or less attractive to different individuals. Again, this is a factor which only you can decide on, but it is something which will impact heavily on your life at university.

Home or Away?

Increasingly, with the growth of the universities in the United Kingdom, higher education is available near to home. You may be able to continue living at home while studying, though this depends on where you live and what courses a local university offers. A number of Catholic institutions now offer distance-learning degrees which have the advantage of flexibility about where you live. For many, higher education means moving away from home, usually for the first time; but this does not suit everyone. You might not want to leave behind your family, friends and familiarity – and there is nothing wrong with this. It may also be that you are constrained financially and living at home is a cheaper option. I know of many students living in the South East for whom commuting daily into London is the only way they can afford to study there.

Money – or lack of it

Financial issues are playing an ever larger role in choosing a university. Student loans and the increasing levels of debt can put an enormous burden on individuals and families. Whatever we feel about these government policies, they are an influential reality for most students. In choosing a course or place, this must always be taken into considera-tion and carefully thought through. Part-time, distance-learning courses offer a cheaper route, and mean that you can combine study with earning money.

At some stage you will need to repay what you have borrowed. This should not condition what or even whether you study, but it should always be at the back of your mind.

University and beyond

By the time you come to leave school or college you may have no idea what path you wish to take in life; I certainly didn't, and most students these days don't either. No longer do we have a course mapped out for us in life, and it may be that we have to change our job several times. As society develops rapidly, so our responses within it change.

STUDENT VIEW: Confidence and uncertainty

I had long known that I wanted to study music at university, but the choice of which universities to apply to was a strange one. I hadn't even managed to get hold of any prospectuses by last September, and then when I did look at them they left me even more confused. The prospectuses were useful for course information and for facilities, but not a lot else – each one claimed to offer the best music course around! This was not much use in helping me to choose between them.

So I've had to rely on outside knowledge and have taken advantage of family connections, friends and contacts. Friends in York, Durham and Cambridge have all been helpful. It's taken some doing, but then if I'd only relied on information from prospectuses and open days, I'd still be none the wiser about where to go.

As well as looking at the courses and the universities, I've also tried to find out about what the Catholic life is like within each university. I want to practise my faith there, so I'll need some kind of support, given the prevailing climate. Chaplaincy websites are helpful and I've picked out a few where I think I might fit in. I haven't finally decided on which offers to accept and which to refuse, but there are more pressing matters to worry about – like actually getting my 'A' Levels!

Matthew Ward, Whitby, North Yorkshire

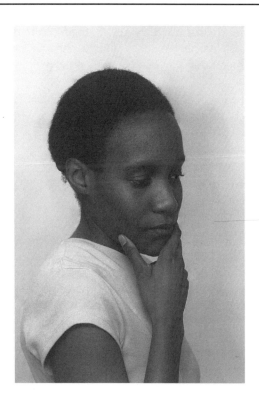

Certain university courses are quite clearly vocational (such as medicine, engineering, architecture, etc.), but they are not exclusively so; just because you have studied a particular subject, does not condition you to that discipline for life.

It may well be that during your time at university you discover that you are being led in a completely different direction – an English student I know who is due to graduate this year has had a complete change and now wants to start again with a degree in medicine. Indeed, it is often only through our time at university that we discover what God wants us to do with our lives. Our study, our social and spiritual lives, and the developments we undergo during this time all contribute to this discernment.

"Where's the best place for a Catholic?"

The final factor that you will need to consider is the impact of university on your faith. It is true that the lack of Catholic universities in the UK does make it harder for a Catholic student to discern where his or her faith may best grow. There are, of course, a few Catholic colleges of higher education (these are all listed in Part II of the Guide), but you are still more likely than not to find yourself attending a secular university.

This does not mean that your faith has to suffer. Nearly all the universities have a Catholic chaplain assigned to them to facilitate Catholic student life. It is within the context of this environment, which features a welcoming and youthful Catholic community, that many students truly discover their faith. You can be as involved or not as you like – and in many ways this decision is going to be determined by, and will impact on, your faith much more than your choice of university. Wherever you go, there will be the opportunity for you to practise and live out your faith.

Even allowing for this, though, you may find that you are more suited to the Catholic life at one university or college than another. So visit the chaplaincy when you are attending an Open Day to see what is going on. As one prospective student, Matthew, describes on the previous page, his faith is certainly a factor in his choice of where to go to university.

Limited choices

All of these factors provide a framework in which to choose where to go, but we do not live in a perfect world. Sometimes you will not be entirely free to make the choice that you would like. For a number of reasons, you might find that you cannot have your first choice of course or university. It may be that you have not got the right grades, in which case you might wish to re-sit certain exams. Financial considerations may also be relevant: that you don't wish to bear the burden of such a heavy student loan, and living at home is the only option.

Whatever the reason, it is vitally important that you are happy and comfortable with whatever you eventually choose – that you do not see it as a "second-best". Often what we initially perceive as second-best is in fact right for us. There is absolutely no point going to study at a place where you will not be able to cope academically; it will only make your time at university a complete burden. This can mean swallowing your pride and accepting the reality of the situation. Making the right choice is about looking for the place where you can come to your fullest potential, not simply trying for the most prestigious university.

Advice versus pressure

For some, parental pressure will also be an issue. You should try both to be as free as possible to choose for yourself, and to be aware that parental pressure is completely distinct from parental *advice*. You should always seek advice from as many different sources as possible – this is one of the ways that we truly come to make informed decisions in life. Your teachers, careers advisors, parish priest, school chaplain, friends, family and parents will often have the experience and wisdom to help you choose sensibly.

You do need to understand the difference between encouragement and pressure: your parents are usually the people who know you best and want what is best for you. Some students who come to my own university, Oxford, mention having felt

pressurised to apply; but they have more usually been encouraged along by people who, knowing them, knew that it would be the right study environment for them (sometimes before the students themselves were willing to admit it).

What happens if it all goes wrong?

It can, however, become apparent quite early on in university life that you have made the wrong choice. You may find yourself unable to cope intellectually, or unhappy emotionally, socially or spiritually. In this case it is essential to share your feelings with those who are close to you and those responsible for your study, and perhaps also with a chaplain. More often than not this is a temporary phase which most students experience at some point. Sometimes you can change a course quite easily, or put on hold your study to return the following year. In other cases it may be important to accept the reality of the situation and to leave the university altogether. You can always apply again the following year to study either a different subject or in a different place. Or it may be appropriate to find employment and return to university at some considerably later date. All of this requires honesty and courage. What is important is that you don't consider this a failure: different things suit and are intended for different people at different times in their lives.

So where does my faith fit into it all?

Ultimately, Catholics should always choose in the light of their faith. Your choice will be moulded by a number of issues, both practical and more personal, and it ought to be the result of informed thought. You have the freedom to use your reason: so discern, reflect and then choose. But this must always be in the context of a relationship with God – a relationship nourished by prayer, reading the Bible and living a sacramental life. As one student puts it:

> I didn't do a tour of chaplaincies when looking around campuses to see which was the friendliest, but I'd still say that my faith played a fundamental role in the decision-making process. Prayer was key in helping me discover what it was that I was looking for out of my time at university, but it was also important in helping me to make sense of all the advice and information I was getting.

This indeed is a key time for you to call on God in prayer: he loves us, knows us, and will guide us along our individual path. In this way you can be sure that you will make the best possible choice.

TAKING A GAP YEAR
Susan Holloway

Only recently I found myself with my own theatre production organised at the school where I taught English, a range of friends from over a dozen countries, and a brand new way of life. Had someone told me a couple of months ago that I would be doing all of this in a foreign country, I simply would not have believed them. All of this has been part of the gap year that I am still taking even as I write. I left school only a few months ago, and university is still on the horizon for me.

Why go for it?

Many other young people find themselves in a similar position. After all, gap years are becoming increasingly common. But perhaps the hardest aspect to taking a gap year is making the decision in the first place. People obviously question it and ask: *Why take a year out?* I faced a huge dilemma, but very late on in my last year at school I eventually decided to go for it. The reasons for taking a gap year all stacked up for me. Looking back I can see now that these reasons centre on discovering the person inside and exploring the world outside. After so many years of education, I also felt that it would be good to have a break from the routine of study to refresh myself. It is only too easy to feel trapped at home, both physically and psychologically – you have been under the eye of your parents all your life. So it is a new experience to be independent, and during a year out you can make the most of this freedom.

Inside and outside

Taking a gap year can offer you a great deal. Whether working, travelling or learning a new skill, the benefits are enormous in terms of self-confidence, independence and knowledge. If you take on paid work, the financial side evidently has its advantages. It can be a great boost at university in helping to pay for tuition fees, accommodation and food. You also learn about the world of work and can add experience to your chosen university course. If you travel to another corner of the globe, then you experience a different culture. You could learn a new language, either in this country or on a stay abroad, a stay that might range from a few weeks to a few months. Or you could use the year to pursue hidden interests in art, drama and music,

STUDENT VIEW: The 'Mother Teresa' experience

Last year, when I came to organise my year abroad as part of my degree, I wanted to use it to discover what volunteer work in a developing country was like. Basically, I wanted the "Mother Teresa" experience in a Spanish-speaking country. So I arranged to teach English in a small town in Latin America.

As I first explored the town where I would be living, I saw virtually nothing that was familiar – there were no shop signs, no W H Smith, no supermarket – nothing that communicated to me where I could buy all the day-to-day things. On my first Sunday there, the couple I was living with took me to the local market and invited me to pick Sunday lunch from the cages of live chickens and rabbits. I will never forget the rabbit grabbed by its ears and shoved into a shopping bag! As I walked down the street, everyone would stare because they were so unused to seeing a white, tall, "gringa" (foreigner). The house where I was staying was simple, and again, it took some time to adjust to things. There was no hot water, and each morning I would dread stepping under the dribble of a shower. There was no washing machine, so my clothes used to pile up until I could find a good length of time to wash them all by hand.

Perhaps we are used to hearing of these types of situations in developing countries and they don't surprise us. What I found on arrival was that they challenged me far more than I had expected. They were all part of a lesson I had to learn in detachment – detachment from the easy way of doing things, from *my* world of *my* things. I realised that this is what Jesus means when he says: "Blessed are the poor in spirit, for theirs is the Kingdom of God." (*Matthew* 5:3)

I discovered this in part from a friend I made while I was there. Odalis is one of thirteen brothers and sisters. I lived with her aunt and uncle and she often stayed overnight with us. She rarely invited me to her house, and when she did I never saw further than her front room which was bare apart from two chairs her father had made. She explained to me how the children all shared beds and how there were curtains dividing the boys from the girls. When Christmas was approaching, she said that the older siblings were out working for the money to make a special meal on Christmas Day. I think of her often now I'm back at university in Britain. I see so much money spent on drink, CDs, inflatable furniture, etc., and yet you hear the constant complaint about student debt. Rather than accumulate objects, I now want to get rid of the many superfluous things I don't really need.

Nicola Waite, recent graduate in English Lit. and Hispanic Studies from Sheffield University or gain extra experience before going on to study them at university.

Volunteer work, though, perhaps holds out the most valuable reward, since it can give you scope to try something you may not be able to do otherwise, whether it's muddy army training in the Peak District or, much more challenging, working with the poor or the sick. It is often easier to try out in a voluntary capacity your future career as a teacher, journalist or carer. There are numerous volunteer projects around Britain ranging from helping children with special needs to providing support for young teenagers. You can even travel around schools and parishes, using drama and music to speak to others about the Catholic faith. These projects all offer an eye-opening experience of the outside world – and we have them on our very doorstep.

In addition, voluntary work overseas offers you the chance to immerse yourself in a completely new culture and this exposure to a different set of values can help you discover an alternative perspective on life. This was what Nicola found, as she describes in the *Student View* on the page opposite. Rather than seeing the problems of developing countries, for example, through the sympathetic and maybe distant eyes of the media, you have the chance to go in person and actually help through concrete actions, rather than just giving money. You will then be living out the advice in the Bible: "Little children, let us not love in word or speech but in deed and truth" (1 Jn 3:18).

Working abroad with people in need is a way of showing this love. It can also affect us in ways that we don't expect. We may set off thinking we are going to give and, although this may be true in a material sense, we discover how much more we have to learn. First-hand exposure to the way billions of people face up every day to unimaginable hardships, reveals the truth that a person's dignity is not dependent on his or her material wealth.

Growth in faith

Another benefit that a gap year can offer is the chance to question and confirm your beliefs. What we believe does affect who we are on the inside. Perhaps for the first time, you find yourself outside the safe circle of life at home. You can no longer rely on family members going with you to Church each week. You are suddenly alone out there and hence the test on your faith is much stronger. What will happen if it is difficult to get to Mass on Sunday? Who will I turn to for back-up?

If you find creative ways to deal with these challenges you will see that your faith deepens. Everyone experiences doubt, but what better way to discover faith than by finding it in the most unlikely circumstances with which you are confronted during a gap year?

What do you want?

Once I had decided to go for it, I then hit the next stage: *What should I do?* I had thought about teaching as a career, enjoyed being with children, and wanted to learn Spanish in an environment with young people. So as things turned out, after looking around and making plenty of phone calls, I found myself teaching English in southern Spain – with no knowledge of Spanish and no knowledge of teaching.

You do need to be clear about what you want from a gap year, whether it be the knowledge of another language, an amazing range of friends

---

STUDENT VIEW: God is so good!

My first experience of Christianity since the age of 14 – when I had stopped going to church with my parents – was during my gap year, which I spent as a volunteer in a L'Arche community[1] for those with disabilities, in Cork. When I first arrived I was surprised to find I was the only non-Catholic, never mind unbeliever, in the community. Through sharing in the life and prayer of the community I found faith in God, and one day I admitted: "Okay, I believe in You". From then on I had a lot to learn.

I came to university thinking that I'd enjoyed life so far, but that now I could stop going to those dull Catholic churches I had encountered in my gap year, and join the Christian Union. So I did, but I was still shocked and upset to feel something missing. I made excuses for the emptiness until one day I was walking past the Catholic Chaplaincy, and saw from the sign outside that Mass was starting in five minutes. Mass felt just right, perhaps because it was so familiar, and I had already decided I would come back – when someone mentioned lunch.

Soon my life revolved around the Chaplaincy – and lectures, of course! I was amazed to meet funny, happy, normal young people who followed (what I saw as) the "restrictive" guidelines of the Church. I gradually came to Mass more and more often – instead of arriving in time for lunch! – and spoke with people who showed me how beautiful the Church's teachings really are.

When I finally realised God was calling me into the Catholic Church, I was surprised at how delighted everyone was! The community in Cork held a special prayer service for me, even though I'd left them 15 months before. Friends arranged for Masses to be said for me in Lourdes, Glastonbury and in the Third World. Because I am still learning, our Church's teachings seem so exciting! I didn't think life could get any better than in L'Arche, but university can be such a blessed time. God is so good!

Mhari Dunlop, undergraduate student in Physiotherapy at the University of Manchester across the world, a renewal of your faith, or simply experience of the world of work. You need to think clearly about the ways in which the year will be valuable. Will teaching English in India really be much help to a medical degree, and what impression would it make on admissions tutors and ultimately your employers? However, provided that you set out with a clear aim in mind, you are guaranteed to learn a lot from taking a year out. It is no surprise that even the top universities typically look favourably on a well-spent gap year.

It is easy to be swept away with visions of backpacking around South America; so it is vital that you think seriously about what you are hoping to gain from it and how you can help others. In choosing from the many possibilities open to you, it is important to remember that God can be your guide; only he knows what is best for you. So why not take some time praying in order to discern what you are trying to achieve?

Plan, Plan, Plan

You do, of course, need to take some initiative when planning a gap year. The organisation of the year is the hardest part, but there are many people and organisations who are happy to help you make the best decision. Apart from the internet, the Gap Year listings in this Guide are a good place to start, as are your own personal contacts. Some organisations, despite the often high prices, offer fantastic opportunities to experience a life which you never knew existed. Organisations such as "Gap Challenge", "I-to-I", and "Teaching Abroad"[2] send their students all over the world.

Even with all of this support available, a gap year has to be thought through carefully in order to ensure that you get the most out of the time and are able to help others during this year. Otherwise it is easy to spend the year drifting or doing very little. In particular, it is likely that earning

money will be important. Most students find that at some point during their gap year they need to earn money, at the very least in order to support their year out. It is expensive to travel the world, and working on a voluntary project usually requires funding, although some voluntary work opportunities do provide you with a living for the year. These practical considerations do have to be taken into account.

If your gap year is taken before university, part of the planning will include getting ready for university the following year. Schools, for instance, usually advise students who want to take a gap year to apply for deferred entry to university. Ideally the gap year will relate in some way to your chosen course. In my own case, I am going to study

French and Spanish at the University of Sheffield; and I didn't know a word of Spanish before embarking on the gap year.

Finally, it is important in your planning to take account of the impact of the gap year on your faith. Organisations such as those named above are, of course, non-denominational, so, for someone travelling with one of them, extra thought would need to go into how to ensure the practice of one's faith does not suffer for the sake of a bit of adventure. You need to be prepared to take some initiative, being up-front about your needs at an early stage. On the other hand, there are many organisations within the Church that offer fantastic opportunities abroad, so that you can travel the globe, meet new people, and explore who you really are in an environment which will nurture and support your faith.[3] You may well find it surprising how much a gap year can impact on your faith, as Mhari did after spending a year living alongside adults with disabilities (see previous page).

Seize the opportunity!

In our parents' generation, hardly anyone would have had the chance to choose from such a wide variety of options. We are capable of providing so much help to others, help that is both spiritual and physical; and we in turn have so much support open to us, through our parents, schools, colleges, organisations, the internet, books, magazines and much more. We should count ourselves extremely privileged. My advice to you is to broaden your horizons and to seriously consider taking a gap year.

Notes

[1] For details of L'Arche, see p. 97.

[2] For details of such organisations, see the listing of internet addresses, p. 110.

[3] Details of these organisations are included under the 'Gap Year' listings in Part II of the Guide p. 95.

FINDING ACCOMMODATION
Fiorella Sultana de Maria

A colleague once told me about an Italian friend of hers who had gone to study at an American university. His name was Nicola and he had not been settled in his hall of residence long before he realised that the only students he could see milling around were women – giving him extremely funny looks. He soon realised that his name appeared to be female in English, and he had inadvertently been put in a female hall of residence!

Finding decent accommodation at university is obviously vitally important for those leaving home, but it is an area of life that new students often spend little time thinking about. The fact is that where you live determines a great deal about the friends you make, the amount of freedom you have to study and socialise, and the level of comfort and security you can enjoy. Moving away from home can be either traumatic or exciting. Whatever it is, though, it will mean a significant change of lifestyle, and it is important to get it right. So it is worth taking a close look at the main types of accommodation available for Catholic students:

- halls of residence;
- renting and sharing with friends;
- accommodation organised on a Catholic basis.

Living in a Hall of Residence

Living in hall is an excellent way to meet other people and to get used to university life. There is a saying that a student spends his or her three years at university trying to ignore the friends made in Freshers' Week! Whilst this is not always true, it does take time to build up a circle of friends. Most of the people you meet in the first week will not be in it, but they *will* be your colleagues for a number of years, so it is worth being on friendly terms with them as far as possible.

So make the most of the opportunity to meet the people on your staircase or corridor. Even if your room is small and the cooking facilities are verging on the hazardous, it is still possible to invite a few people round for coffee. Always have food and drink in reserve for visitors – it helps to make you a generous host.

You might also keep an eye out for new students who are finding the transition to university traumatic. A surprising number of freshers struggle with homesickness in their first weeks. On my first day at university, I knocked on a girl's door to enquire about a meeting and she burst into tears on me. My reaction was practically to run for my life, and I regretted afterwards that I had not kept my nerve and made an effort to cheer her up. The Gospel reminds us over and over again of the need to take care of others. There is no need to be overbearing or an Agony Aunt, just being there will be sufficient.

There is, of course, more to life in hall than meeting people, and some forward planning can make a big difference. One advantage of living in hall is that it usually means living in the thick of student life and being conveniently close to university facilities. So find out where your hall is situated – if it is miles away from the main campus, it may be worth finding alternative accommodation.

STUDENT VIEW: My own experience

My first roommate was extremely nice, but it was clear from almost the word go that we had been spectacularly mismatched. We had filled in a questionnaire about ourselves before arriving so that we could be paired up with suitable people, but all that we seemed to have in common was that neither of us smoked cigarettes and we had both taken a gap year – though she had gone to India and I had worked in the Holy Land. It was very funny when we began decorating the room, because her walls were covered in pictures of Hindu deities, and mine were covered with icons and rosaries.

What I was not prepared for, though, was to be cross-examined about my personal beliefs. When a Catholic student came round for tea, we were overheard talking about abortion and, after the friend had left, I was immediately put on the spot. When I said I was pro-life there was an awkward pause. "But you do believe it's the woman's right to choose, don't you?" "No." – Why, I was barely civilised! Welcome to university, I thought, where you can believe what you like as long as you do not dissent beyond certain limits.

I learnt to ignore the noise of my room-`mate coming in late, as she tried to ignore the sound of me getting up for early lectures. Three weeks into term, however, it just became too much and she moved out. It was an amicable parting. In spite of our differences we had become friends, but it was better for both of us to have our privacy.

By the time I finished my undergraduate study, I decided to rent a house with a couple of Catholic friends. As a graduate student, I appreciated being able to go back to a house at the end of the day. It was such a luxury to be able to close the front door behind me and cook dinner with my friends. The house wasn't an escape from the rigours of student life, but it was a private space we could return to when we needed it.

Meanwhile, whereas some halls of residence are clean, spacious and comfortable, others are drab and ill-equipped. If you get the chance to go to an Open Day beforehand, take a look at the accommodation on offer and decide whether you can live with it for any length of time. Old and prestigious universities do not necessarily have universally excellent rooms – check them out first if you can, and bring plenty of posters/hangings/ornaments to liven up the place. Even a relatively unattractive room can be made bearable with a little effort.

Find out beforehand whether or not you will have to share. In some cases, if you do have to share you will be sent a questionnaire before arrival asking about your preferences, in order to try and match you up with an appropriate person. In my experience, this seldom works and it can be very difficult sharing with a stranger, particularly if you have different timetables, tastes and beliefs. The only similarities between myself and my room-mate were that neither of us smoked and we had both taken gap years, as you can gather from my own experience in the *Student View* on the page opposite. Give it some time and if it does not work out, look for an alternative.

Then, on Day One find out who you can turn to for advice or to complain in the event of any problems. Some universities assign students to tutors or supervisors, or there may be a warden who deals with student concerns. If you have a problem with your room, your neighbours or your room-mate, then talk to your warden or another member of staff. It will often be possible to sort out difficulties diplomatically once the concern is raised, either by a simple room swap or by negotiation with the appropriate parties.

Renting and Sharing

An option that many students have to consider, particularly in the second and third years of a degree,

is sharing a privately rented house. Living with friends can be great fun and a huge source of support, bringing with it good company, conversation and the feeling of living in a family. With your own kitchen, it is also possible to entertain friends from elsewhere in the university more easily.

If you choose to share with Catholic friends, or friends who are sympathetic to the Catholic faith, it perhaps means being able to say grace together at mealtimes, get the house blessed, and join together for prayer if timetables allow. It might also mean being able to get up for a glass of water in the night without having to climb over the bodies of assorted visitors of the opposite sex!

Actually finding somewhere to live is the first challenge. Some universities will have accommodation services offering advice and possible places to rent, and university common rooms and notice boards can be good sources of information. Letting agencies will sometimes refuse to take on student clients, but the majority will, and it is generally advisable to go through an agency rather than making a private agreement. If you are renting several years into your course, you will have had the chance to make friends and to group with people whom you know, and with whom you will be happy to live for an extended period of time. Some general points to remember are:

- Always find out about the area in which the house is situated, what the neighbourhood is like, whether it is a safe area to walk through at night, etc.

- Always view the house beforehand. A property that looks promising on paper can prove to have all kinds of hidden problems. Take a good look around. If you are viewing in the summer, try to imagine what the house will feel like in December – Are there draughts? Is the central heating sufficient? Ask plenty of questions.

- Always read the tenancy agreement. It is as much there to protect your rights as the landlord's.

The "evil landlord" stereotype is a little unfair, but some do attempt to take advantage of students, so stand up for yourself. My letting agency had no scruples whatsoever about forcing us to use a faulty gas cooker for a year, and delaying calling someone out for forty-eight hours when our carbon monoxide detector showed dangerous levels of the gas in the house. Getting to know a little about the law surrounding renting worked wonders. Make sure you know your rights as a tenant and do not be afraid to be pushy. If the house is poorly maintained, complain; if appliances are old-fashioned and hazardous, threaten legal action – you have a right to live in a safe environment. If your landlord is bullying or attempts to fob you off, fight back!

Residential Chaplaincies

Living in a Catholic environment can be very encouraging and may provide spiritual as well as social support in the mêlée of a largely hedonistic university existence. Various chaplaincies offer accommodation and, since they are usually fairly small, they can make for friendly and informal places. They will typically have shared common areas, cooking facilities, a chapel and resident chaplain, and offer the opportunity for regular mass attendance. The chaplaincy may also provide opportunities to learn more about your faith, as well as social activities such as parties and film nights, which can offer entertainment after an essay crisis. My chaplaincy provided everything from breakfast and regular prayer during exam time to fancy dress parties – the photographic evidence from which could wreck any number of flourishing careers! Details of residential chaplaincies are provided in the second part of this book.

Whereas small Catholic communities can be friendly, there is often the tendency towards cliquishness. Avoid getting into ghettoes; if you live in an exclusively Catholic environment, make sure that you have social circles in other areas. Also, it is easy to assume that all Catholics share the same views, and if the atmosphere is too conservative, liberal, or apathetic for you, it will not be a supportive environment to live in. Find out about the ethos of the residence before making a decision; talk to people who live there, make an appointment to meet the chaplain.

Lay Communities and other Religious Houses

Some religious congregations in areas where there is a high student population offer rooms to Catholic students. However, priories and convents seldom advertise, so it is a good idea to phone round the religious houses in the area to ask if it would be possible to rent a room. Living in a religious house involves more than simply renting some space. It means, moreover, living as part of a religious community and sharing in the life of the congregation. Depending upon the individual community, you may be expected to attend daily Mass and Divine Office with them, to join them for meals and to help out with the cooking and gardening. It should be seen as a whole experience rather than as a housing option, and it will have a considerable impact upon your life while you are there.

Living as part of a community can be a rewarding experience, particularly (but by no means exclusively) if you are considering the religious life. It offers a stable, structured existence in what can otherwise be a chaotic student lifestyle; the opportunity for spiritual growth; and the security and friendship that a good community spirit can offer. A friend of mine spent a number of years living in a Dominican lay community and, though he discovered (quite early, I think) that he certainly was not destined for ordination, he lived among extraordinary people and gained insights into religious life that he would never otherwise have had.

Community life is not for everyone, however, and can seem intrusive or claustrophobic if you are used to living alone. You will also need to make a commitment to the community, even if only for a short period of time. If you find structured living oppressive rather than helpful, and if you don't relish having to be up for seven-thirty every morning, this option will not be for you.

Finding a home

Wherever you find yourself living during your time at university, make the most of the environment in which you find yourself. Your university or college will be your home for three or more years, and it is important that you live in a way that allows you to be comfortable and safe, and to flourish spiritually, emotionally and mentally.

STUDY
Fr Joseph Evans

When my mother was a schoolteacher in Nigeria in the 1950s, one of her jobs was to go through the library at the end of the day to flush out pupils hiding under the bookshelves. Such was the thirst for learning among these young Africans that they sought to be locked into the library, to spend the whole night studying. In a subsequent school, her pupils were non-boarders who often walked miles to get to classes, rising at the crack of dawn. By the afternoon, fatigue began to show but, rather than snooze in lectures, the tired students would simply stand and continue the rest of the lesson on their feet. My mother was always somewhat disconcerted, but at the same time deeply moved, by these powerful young men towering over her with such interest as she explained English grammar to them.

I imagine that most of us would need to be locked *into* a library rather than excluded from one, such is the natural resistance we feel to getting down to serious study. But those young Nigerians can teach us a lesson: they were so keen to learn because they saw in study a means to get on, and were therefore prepared to make the necessary sacrifices.

Why study?

Of course, sacrifices are necessary for study. Hence the Bible seems to sympathise with bored students forced to suffer a tedious lecture on a hot Friday afternoon. We read in the book of Ecclesiastes (1:18)

> "For in much wisdom is much vexation, and he who increases knowledge increases sorrow"

In general, however, the overall Biblical view of wisdom is highly favourable: it is worth acquiring as a *good in itself*. This is in contrast to some contemporary attitudes to learning whereby knowledge must be *practical*. Some people, for example, are only prepared to study hard if it means that they can get a good job and become rich. Knowledge for knowledge's sake is seen as a luxury that modern society can no longer afford.

In this chapter, I hope to propose a middle way between ancient and modern views of learning. Wisdom is valuable in itself, but it must also be practical, in the sense that it must be inspired by a spirit of service. Put simply, we study for ourselves and for others. What is more, as I will explain,

study can actually be a means to grow in your Christian life.

A distracted fireman

Imagine the following: Fred the fireman is one of the nicest guys you could meet – cheerful, helpful, always cracking jokes. If you need someone to join you for a drink, assist you with a computer query, even accompany you on an errand, Fred is your man. He has only one defect: he is not very good at putting out fires. It is not that he does not want to, it is just that he never seems to get round to it. When the alarm rings, he is always busy doing something else: reading a novel, watching an interesting film, engaging in a fascinating conversation. By the time he thinks of putting on his uniform and sliding down the pole, he realises that he has left it too late. Sometimes he still rushes to the scene of the fire and squirts water madly on the blaze to make up for lost time. Occasionally he gets away with it and manages to save the building. Quite often it is a question of too little too late: the former mansion is now a pile of cinders smouldering at his feet.

STUDENT VIEW: Work – the missing piece in the puzzle

After school I did a year out working as a Graphic Designer, and I was invited on a retreat. I met young people who were keen on their faith and who *lived* it. I was attracted by this and got involved. Looking back, it was great and I am thankful. But the general attitude among us was that to be a good Catholic you had to be a bit cut off from normal life so as not to get contaminated. When I first started at university I realised that providence had led me to become a medical student and therefore I needed to do some work, but my studies were not what mattered. My Christian life was basically a box which contained going to Mass, saying prayers and obeying various moral teachings, and to be a good Christian was to go into that box and shut the lid.

But while at university I made a great discovery: I came to see that my work and studies could be a way to God. It opened up a whole new world. Suddenly all other aspects of my life were also becoming Catholic. I was able to pray about normal things: my life became part of my prayer. Prayer, going to Mass, or saying the Rosary were no longer escaping from reality. I needed them because I needed God's grace *for my daily life*. My existence exploded into a Christian *life*, as opposed to seeing

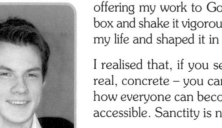

Christianity as *doing certain things*. Through applying myself to my work and offering my work to God, I discovered that being Christian was to open that box and shake it vigorously so that all my Catholicism spilled out into the rest of my life and shaped it in a Christian way.

I realised that, if you seek God through study, your Christian life becomes real, concrete – you can touch it; it's not just a theory. You can understand how everyone can become a saint, and sanctity itself becomes concrete and accessible. Sanctity is not just for the monastery. It is found in everyday life.

Robert Devlin, third-year medical student

Many students are, of course, like Fred. They give time to everything except their books. The days before exams and coursework deadlines are a furious rush to try to make up for weeks of neglect. But while the idea of a forgetful fireman is fanciful, the consequences for students who act like this are very real. And not only for their grades but also for their character. The student who does not study will almost inevitably be lazy, disorganised, weak and immature.

Study is good for you – honest !

The flip-side to this is that careful study is intrinsically good for us. Thus one sees in a responsible student such qualities as perseverance, self-discipline, initiative, the ability to solve problems and to work in a team, the virtue of order, generosity in sharing time and knowledge with others, and so on.

I would further emphasise that not only can study help you to become a better person, it is also *necessary* if you want to have an enjoyable and fulfilling university experience. Serious study gives the necessary framework to student life: without it, everything else falls apart. If, by dedicating oneself *excessively* to having fun or even to some seemingly worthwhile activity, one neglects one's studies, our conscience soon starts to complain (even when the tutors do not, though they soon will).

With study as the backbone of our day, we can slot around it other useful activities, especially those involving helping others (e.g. some voluntary work).

Sport is also positive. It helps us rest and relieves nerves and stress, and thus actually helps us to study better. Then time should be found to develop friendships, a key aspect of university life. In addition, getting involved in some worthwhile university society is beneficial, as is reading good literature and developing other cultural interests. Many students will find that they need to take on paid employment during their studies, but if this takes precedence over everything else you will miss out on so much.

It is not, of course, easy to balance all of these activities. Ideally you should make a general weekly plan, which must then be adapted to each day with a rough timetable and set of targets; try setting a fixed number of hours to study per week. You may often not reach the target, but you will do a lot more study than if you never decided on a goal to aim at. Of course, your daily plan should not include *just* study. It will also include time for all the other activities and time for God.

Study as service

There is another reason to dedicate oneself conscientiously to one's books. Study is a real practical service to society. Speaking to an audience of university students in 2002, Pope John Paul II said:

> "In fact, study and work imply a personal attitude of openness and giving ourselves to others which we call, precisely, 'service' (...) With this openness to your brothers and sisters, each one of you, dear young people, perfects, thanks also to study and to work, fundamental aspects of your own mission, making the talents which God has generously given you bear fruit." [1]

In other words, by studying we develop our talents, which can then be put to use for the welfare of society. It is like an investment in oneself with a view to future service. This approach, while still practical, is quite different from studying in order to get a good job and become rich. And if among Catholics there were many students studying hard, developing effective working habits and getting good grades, there would be more likelihood of some of them later being able to serve society at the top level and bear witness to Christian principles there, as did St Thomas More.

Study and Christian life

So we study for ourselves *and* for others. It would, though, be a mistake to view study as something independent and distinct from the Christian life. We are not Catholics *and* students. One must live one's Catholicism *in* one's study. This is the lesson Robert learned. When he had finished at school, he was a typical "Sunday-Mass Catholic". "I was ready to defend the Church in the pub, and I wouldn't sleep around, but my faith had little impact on my daily life." He tells his story on the previous page.

In living out our faith in our daily life, we also have the example of Christ to guide us. He chose to spend the greater part of his life as a craftsman in Nazareth. Jesus, who came to save and redeem us, also saved us by offering to God his daily sweat in Joseph's workshop. It is like God telling us, "I consider work so important, so good for man, that I dedicated most of my life as a man to working."

Study as work

As students it is our study that is our work. So, following where Christ led, we can offer our study to God ("Lord, I offer you this essay and all the effort it involves"). We can even offer it up for a particular intention ("Lord, take this assignment as a gift and prayer for the health of my uncle Eric"). Thus, for a Catholic student, study can be a form of prayer. Obviously this requires that we study just as well as we can, since it makes no sense to offer second-class gifts to God.

At the same time, though, we also need to pray and frequent the sacraments. Our prayer and our contact with Christ will give us the desire and spiritual "energy" to offer our work to Him. Our work offered up reinforces our prayer life: "I pray for the conversion of my friend, and I want it so much that I also offer the effort of doing a boring essay for this intention." And it is both our life of prayer and our study converted into prayer which gives us the power and grace to offer effective Christian witness, in a natural way, to our friends and colleagues. We will more effectively re-Christianise society by doing our work well and by offering it to God than by any amount of distributing leaflets or organising meetings. Being a good student is in fact a great help in our efforts to be a witness to Jesus, conferring professional standing among our peers. If, on the other hand, we neglect our study, people will find it harder to take us seriously: "a lot of talk about God, but he (or she) never does a stroke of work!"

A deeper knowledge

A final suggestion: try to find time to read about your faith and to deepen your experience of it. Questions and doubts can provide a stimulus for this reading, but so can a growing conviction that our faith is important. There are numerous sound books on the subject. It would be a shame to finish your course with a university-level knowledge of, say, physics, computer systems or English literature, and a primary-school knowledge of your faith. This latter is really the science that matters most, since it opens the door to eternal life.

A great Church Father, St Ambrose, once compared a well-read man to the clouds which fill with water in order to rain upon the earth and make the crops grow. Thus he said: "He who reads much is filled with understanding. He who is filled, waters others." [2] Through our study and reading we can fill ourselves with knowledge and learning which enrich us as persons and which can be put to the service of society as a whole. If you study hard, you will be filled with understanding, and through your wisdom you will help the whole world to become a better place.

Notes

[1] Pope John Paul II, Address to participants in the UNIV 2002 Congress, Rome, 25th March 2002.

[2] St Ambrose of Milan, Letter 2.

"What *am* I doing here?" you ask yourself after a fifty-minute lecture on "Immune-system interactions with phospholipids". But then you remember that life begins on Thursday night ... and that's only three days away! Between now and then you have crucial details to work out. What will you wear, who will be there, and will you do it? Do what? Any of it?

We are writing from our two individual perspectives of university living. All personal perspectives are formed in the middle of life's trials and errors; they are naturally limited because we only have our own experiences to work from. Although not everything included in these pages will resonate with you, we hope that our reflections will help you to give some fresh thought to friendships, pub-crawls, sex, and forgiveness.

A guiding vision

We asked a group of eighteen-year-old girls, "Where do you want to be in ten years' time?" "Married; children; a successful job and sustained friendships; at peace" were just some of the answers. Are these typical responses? Ask yourself the question and see what you come up with.

When you have created a list, realise that you have in front of you only one perspective on the future – this is the future *as you want it to be*. To get the full stereoscopic vision, you also have to try to see things *from God's point of view*. "Before I formed you in the womb I knew you, before you were born I consecrated you." [1] God has a plan for us, and our happiness is deeply rooted in seeking that plan.

In university life, with all its choices and demands, we need the guiding vision of God to get us through. Sometimes the stresses of life narrow our vision, and without realizing it we get caught up in something. The feeling of being caged, or blocked in, can be paralysing. But if we seek God's perspective, things are different. His vision does not cage us in; it opens us out and frees us for creative action.

Friendships

We are always curious about what happens to our friends. It's a natural part of social living. Give us the action-reaction scene and let us judge! Sure, when it's a famous person we seem more interested, but that's because we expect them to act in certain ways. That's what's interesting. Think about it. Without expectations we would never find his action surprising, or smile at her reaction. We have all experienced enough of life to know what *could* happen. And yet, we wait ... will he? ... will she? It's all part of the drama of being human, and we all get entangled in the action without realising it.

But friends equally shape your lifestyle choices. They make you curious. They cause you to wonder about your own decisions and whether they were right. "If he's so happy sleeping around, why aren't I?", or "Perhaps I should try it out." Our friend-

ships confront us with these dilemmas, and, because of them, we are tempted to experiment with our bodies and our souls. We seek to satisfy that inner hunger with new bodily experiences, whether in a club in search of the tracer-filled ecstasy trance or in the bedroom in search of the sexual pleasure and intimacy we see modelled in films. We are constantly challenged by friendships; challenges that can build us up as well as tear us down.

God and the clubbing scene

Cyrus spent his third year at university in an international exchange program in Aberdeen, while I did the same at the University of Innsbruck in Austria. Cyrus was dropped off by his parents at his hall of residence beside the River Dee. As he says,

"My heart sank as they drove away. I knew I had to sort everything out for myself. Memories of friends and family flashed through my head: could I manage without them? But I wasn't allowed too much navel-gazing. Quickly-won friends soon dragged me off to clubs, parties, pubs and foreign countries. I was searching to understand myself; I explored identities through other people, to see where I would fit in. It was then that I discovered drum and bass music and the clubbing scene, the deep

conversations and hot-headed fights of the pubs, the dangers of being too sexually intimate, as well as the depth of the Catholic Church – there I found strong, humble people seeking the vision of God. For me, these experiences are all lumped together, not because they were all good, but because they were all packed into one year and are attached to friends whom I used and treated poorly, to friends who used me and spat me out, and to others who enriched my life and deepened my relationship with God."

Your friends may take you to places where you do not want to go. There is a big difference, however, between a friend who challenges you to open yourself to God or to new cultural experiences, and one who closes you up in the world of your own self by caging you in their addictions. Some will try to introduce you to the latter which they consider their "friends" (cocaine is sometimes referred to in this way when one is first "introduced" to the drug) and you need to be able to see where people are trying to take you. So be aware of this, and be ready to firmly but gently take your stand.

'My policy is yes but not yet'

Sex – my policy is yes ... but not yet!

It took a lot of broken relationships for me (Julie) to realise that they all had one thing in common: no regrets. I never look back at my past relationships and say, "I knew I should have had sex with him." There were other regrets, but sex was never one of them. My policy was, "Yes, but not yet." Yes, I think sex is good, but not in this context. I wanted it all: the love, the romance, the

STUDENT VIEW: Something about Mary

I will never forget the day. The period of time before and after is a blur, but that day, I will never forget. John and I had been together since September, and very seriously; he was my first love. We were having sex from the start. We used condoms . . . well, most of the time.

I still have flashbacks of crying hysterically in the shower and holding my stomach. It was strange, I knew the baby was growing inside me, but I wouldn't let myself even consider anything else. I slept all the time, my parents had no clue; they thought I was ill. I didn't really know anything about abortion. No one had ever sat me down to talk about the facts, what was really happening inside me. All I knew was that it would fix my life and get me back to normal . . . or so I thought.

I had to talk to John. He and I sat in his car, and as the words came out of my mouth, he exclaimed "You're not keeping it are you?" I responded, "No!" I couldn't have the baby and humiliate my family, how could I possibly go through with having it? No, no, no, NO! But panic, stress and confusion filled my life. I was a caged animal and needed the key to get out.

When I went into the clinic they had a radio in the waiting room and a friend and I sat listening to music. A nurse came in and I told her I wanted the strongest anaesthetics possible. They didn't put me completely under, but it was like being drunk. I remember the doctor rushing in; he turned on the vacuum pump and it was done in minutes. He quickly left and that was that. I remember the song that played – to this day, every time I hear the song, I am back in that room.

Then, we were sent to a different room; my friend braided my hair and put some make-up on me. We got up to leave. John was in the waiting room with a dozen roses for me. I was still really out of it from all the medicine. We called my parents and told them we were going out. It was Friday, and the next day was an athletics event . . . one that I was competing in. That night, I can't remember. I woke up the next morning and went to the competition, some two hours away. After every race I went to the loo and cried, but not out of physical pain. I couldn't explain it; I just cried. That night when I got home, I remember falling to my knees crying and I felt I was going crazy. I called John. He came over, but we couldn't talk about it. I have no idea what happened after that, but I do know that I changed. I became a different person. I was no longer socially relaxed and at ease. I lost my spirit! I was free again, but my spirit was gone. Strangely, I had no idea why. John and I separated, and to this day I know that every time he sees me, he thinks of it.

I never revisited this event in my life until I reached university. I learned there what happened from conception to birth, and the horror hit – I had made a big mistake! It was really upsetting and the whole thing came flooding back to me. A friend thought that I should resolve this and see a counsellor. I saw a helpful Catholic counsellor, who spent time praying with me. She encouraged me to learn to forgive myself and others in my life. I told my parents and they grieved with me. They said, "We wish we had known; we would have seen you through it!"

Sex is a gamble. The condom broke; that's how I became pregnant. Somehow I forgot that sex creates babies. The primary reason for sex is to bring new life into the world, so why was I so surprised that I became pregnant? Never think "It won't happen to me", because it can. You might be faced with a pregnancy. In a crisis it is hard to think straight and make the right decision. Your decision to have sex can affect you for the rest of your life.[2]

intimacy, the friendship and the freedom. Even though I didn't always know why, I held on to my virginity because somehow I knew it was the right thing to do. Only over time did I begin to see how free I was by waiting.

One by one, my friends had become sexually involved and had started to experience the caging effect of sex. Couples were attaching themselves emotionally and psychologically without the commitment. Breaking up was then a messy business, often accompanied by depression and heavy drinking. Sexually transmitted diseases, abortion, and cynicism about love were all signs that something had gone seriously wrong, but what? I asked my friend, Mary, to share her story (see previous page). It captures something of the love, pain and heartache of sexual intimacy outside of marriage.

The first port of call

This above all: to thine ownself be true
And it must follow, as the night the day
Thou canst not then be false to any man.
– Shakespeare, *Hamlet*

If we are to sustain any creative vision for our lives, we need to be true to ourselves. And if we are true to ourselves, then we cannot be false to others – Shakespeare got it right. If, however, we lie to ourselves, we cheat ourselves of real happiness. God has placed inside us the first port of call in decision-making: our *conscience*.

What *is* a conscience? "Conscience is man's most secret core, and his sanctuary. There he is alone with God whose voice echoes in his depths."[3] When we listen to our conscience we are able to judge between what is good and what is evil. However, we sometimes make wrong judgments because our conscience is poorly formed. When this happens it is important that we alter our sense of what is good. The more we look upon Jesus,

the more our conscience echoes with his standard of goodness and the more we seek his approval. And no amount of seeking affirmation in pubs, clubs, bedrooms or ballrooms can substitute for the wonderful gift of God's approval.

Can you recall when you were asked to do something against your conscience, when your friends were hoping that the "will he?" and the "will she?" would be followed by that leap into the new – perhaps this drink or that pill? Do you remember? Were you true to yourself above all else? Both of us know that we were not, and every time we folded under the pressure, we drowned out our consciences. Even if we did what our friends wanted us to do, we can still say, like Shakespeare, that we let those same friends down by being false to ourselves.

If you ignore or subvert your conscience, that echoing core at the centre of your person, you are no longer being true to your very self. Instead, be sure to listen; it's there precisely to help you through such moments, so that you can confound the expectations of those around you. God assures us that he doesn't place any challenge, any temptation, in our path without giving us the power to overcome.

Body talk — ways to wear it

We also need to recognise that our sexual behaviour has immense power to thwart or realise our aspirations for the future. Sexual activity deeply affects us, our whole person and our whole lives. During sex we become attached to the other person. As I once heard it said, it's like wrapping tape around your arm, with the tape binding itself to the skin. Adam expressed it perfectly when he looked at Eve and said, "This at last is bone of my bones and flesh of my flesh." [4] It is no wonder that bitterness and emptiness can accompany the breakup of a sexual relationship – when the tape is ripped off, the skin comes away with it.

Physical and emotional bonding go hand-in-hand with another aspect of sex – babies! Babies are a naturally good result of sex. It surprises us how many people are shocked at becoming pregnant through sex, but pregnancy is the *most natural* element of sex. Contraception, because it is so easily accessible, has brought many people to forget this reality. Every person who uses a form of contraception intends to avoid the "baby" factor, but this aspect of sex is never absent. Like our conscience, we can only try to drown it out, because even when a condom or a pill is used, we *know* that we are saying "No" to babies, "No" to our bodies, and "No" to our partner.

The body speaks the language of the soul. Our desire to be loved is not just physical. The human person wants to be loved entirely and faithfully. Especially amongst unmarried people, contraception becomes an escape from commitment and fidelity. When someone feels used they don't say, "He wasn't using me, he was only using my body." The tears follow from the rejection of the whole person. Did you see the images in the media of the SARS virus in China? People were kissing each other goodbye through face masks! Using contraception is like putting a mask between you

and the one you are supposed to love. But who wants to be "protected" and separated from the one you love? Commitment and fidelity mean giving everything, holding nothing back.

But contraception is not the only action that rejects the total gift of the person, body and soul. The language of babies is absent in any homosexual act, and a part of the whole person is thus missing. Yet this language is not cancelled out; our bodies always speak with it because it is part of our whole self and we cannot cut out a part of ourselves without causing harm. That is why the Church preserves the great gift of sex for marriage, because it is the only place where the body can speak freely and openly towards the creation of new life.

A further effect of sex occurs on the spiritual level, the level of the heart and soul. God made us in his image; God is love, and God gave us sex to imitate his love. This is why vows, whether religious or marital, are so important for spiritual life. Spiritual joy and fulfilment can only come through the surrender of our whole person to God and others in committed love. Broken relationships, loneliness, infidelity, abortion, sexually transmitted diseases, etc. are all signs of misdirected love. Instead of being complete and whole we are broken into pieces, without the ability to heal ourselves.

Forgiveness – The Heart of the Matter

> I've been trying to get down
>   to the Heart of the Matter
> But my will gets weak
>   and my thoughts seem to scatter
> But I think it's about forgiveness, forgiveness
> Even if you don't love me anymore.

These words, from a fantastic song by Don Henley called "The Heart of the Matter", sum up the best advice we could give to anyone who has been

through a painful relationship. Seek forgiveness and give forgiveness. The whole of Jesus' mission is about the power of love that heals and cleanses our spirit. God's love takes away the weight of guilt.

One of the most important encounters with God during my university life was in the confessional. Never was the power of Jesus felt so strongly as in the words, "Through the ministry of the Church I grant you pardon and peace, and I absolve you of your sins in the name of the Father, and of the Son and of the Holy Spirit." Sometimes I left the confessional and wept out of joy. At other times I felt still and quiet, but in that space I knew I had been forgiven forever.

St. Paul tells us that nothing can separate us from the love of God. If we trust God enough, no matter how often we fail, God can make us whole again. Cyrus and I failed often during our time at university. We have offered a few reflections here which may help you on your journey, and we leave you with these words from Pope John Paul II:

> Dear young people: do not be afraid of honest effort and honest work; do not be afraid of the truth. With Christ's help, and through prayer, you can answer his call, resisting temptations and fads, and every form of mass manipulation. Open your hearts to the Christ of the Gospels – to his love and his truth and his joy. Do not go away sad! [5]

Notes

[1] *Jeremiah* 1:5
[2] Pregnancy counselling is available from LIFE (see p. 105), as well as from other organisations.
[3] Second Vatican Council, *Gaudium et Spes*, 16.
[4] *Genesis* 2:23
[5] Homily on Boston Common, 1 October 1979.

University is often the first time that we are really free to make choices for ourselves. Certainly, it will be a time when there are many changes to the way we live. Student life is, however, rarely lacking in opportunities for quick fixes – drugs, alcohol abuse, short-term sexual relationships – but these temporary highs do not fulfil us and lead instead to emptiness and disappointment.

At a time like this, our relationship with God is more important than ever. As we come to know God more closely we will be better able to make choices that lead to genuine fulfilment, but in order to develop this friendship with God we have to use our freedom positively and give time to prayer, to our encounter with him.

Perhaps, though, you find it difficult to pray regularly. Indeed, people often think of prayer as something you only do before an exam or after a close relative has died. These are times when we experience first-hand both our weakness and our need for God's help, but the reality is that we need God's help all of the time, as the human rights campaigner James Mawdsley realised in an appalling prison in Burma. Even when his protests against the inhumanity of prison life were at their strongest, he began to understand that he was still utterly weak and doomed to failure without God.

Think about your own life. Is it difficult to go and talk to someone who is off on their own, and wearing the wrong clothes? Is it easy to get angry when your milk is stolen from the fridge? Without God, the reality is that we are incapable of loving others.

Five ways of praying

We need to find ways to pray that actually work for us. To aid us in this search, it is worth listening to some advice from Pope John Paul II. He recently recommended to young people five particular ways of praying: personal prayer, meditation on Scripture, Mass, Eucharistic Adoration and the Sacrament of Reconciliation.[1]

It helps to think of **personal prayer** as a conversation with the Lord: thank and praise him; ask for his help; and pray for others. A great way to begin the day is to raise it to God in prayer. Or you can slip into your local church or chaplaincy and just kneel down. There is no

need to worry about *how* to pray. All that matters is that we *do* pray. After all, it is the Holy Spirit who leads our prayer, who "helps us in our weakness" when we "do not know how to pray as we ought" (*Romans* 8:26).

On countless occasions, **Bible readings** have been a source of light and good advice for us. In times of great distress, for example, we have found psalms which have mirrored our own feelings exactly. The discovery that the psalmists turned to God with the whole range of raw human emotion makes us realise that we are not alone: people have turned to God in desperation for thousands of years. It also gives us real hope: the psalmists displayed the depth of their faith, frequently praising God for his endless compassion. Meanwhile, the Gospels are at the heart of the Bible, since they focus on the life of Jesus, and reading and reflecting on them will help us to know Jesus better. Why not find a friend and read together just a small Gospel passage each day?

The Mass is the greatest prayer of all. In the Mass, bread and wine become the Body and Blood of Christ. Constrained by our human limitations, we cannot fully understand how amazing this is, but, each time we go to Mass, we are invited to *actually receive* our risen Lord, who wishes to feed us with his own Self so that he might "raise our mortal bodies and make them like his own in glory".[2] If we think of it in these terms, Mass will never seem boring again, and maybe we will also find time to get to Mass during the week.

Jesus remains present in the Blessed Sacrament, which is

reserved with honour in every tabernacle. Sometimes, the consecrated Host is placed in a monstrance for a time of prayer. **Eucharistic Adoration** is a most intimate experience of Jesus' presence; in a sense, it is the mystery of the Mass suspended for our contemplation. Mother Teresa explained: "I make a Holy Hour each day in the presence of Jesus in the Blessed Sacrament. All my sisters in the Missionaries of Charity make a daily Holy Hour as well, because we find that through our daily Holy Hour, our love for Jesus becomes more intimate, our love for each other more understanding and our love for the poor more compassionate." Many churches will have set times of Eucharistic Adoration; in others, it may be possible to arrange this with your priest.

We can all feel weighed down by our sins and failings. The **Sacrament of Reconciliation** gives us the opportunity to have that burden lifted and to begin again. The purpose of this sacrament is the forgiveness of our sins and, as the name indicates, our reconciliation both with God and with all creation. It is often known as "Confession", though our admission of sins forms only one part of it; the real emphasis should be on God's mercy. The priest is not there to condemn us; he is there – in God's name – to set us free. Priests are rarely shocked even by the confession of serious sins, but there is no need to have committed some big sin in order to make use of the Sacrament of Reconciliation. Regular use of this sacrament helps us to look at all the little things that get in the way of our capacity to love. We would urge anyone who is hesitating to take courage and give it another go!

Beyond childhood faith

We can benefit from all of these ways of praying, but what we *believe* also has an impact on the choices that we make, and thus on whether we end up looking for quick fixes or for true fufilment. Many of us acquire our beliefs as children and have most of our Catechism classes before our First Holy Communion and Confirmation. Whilst important, this is rarely followed by much further instruction in our faith. At university, we might be challenged by new lifestyles and by problems which our childhood faith neither encompasses nor explains. We might feel tempted to rebel against teachings of the Church that we hardly understand. So we should be ready to ask searching questions to *inform* our understanding; the Catholic chaplaincy is one place for such discussions.

We, ourselves, are convinced that the Catholic Church, founded by Jesus Christ and guided by the Holy Spirit, has been able to reveal the truth

---

STUDENT VIEW: Witness

We were standing outside the university hospital, praying. People passed us by in the dark. I'd been reluctant to get involved. After all, we were holding a prayer vigil in front of a place where we believed abortions took place. Any of my friends might have seen me there. Who knows what they might have thought?

I wouldn't normally have gone in for this kind of thing, but a few months before I'd been to a Youth 2000 Prayer Festival. We were all praying in front of the Blessed Sacrament when I caught sight of a mother playing quietly with her little son, right near to the Sacrament. It was the most beautiful sight I have ever seen. At that moment I realised that I could no longer stand aside in the face of abortion.

Then when I started university earlier this year I joined the pro-life society[3]. The society welcomes anyone, whatever their faith or background, who wants to witness to the reality that an abortion kills a child. Not that we've had a lot of time to do much. Pressures of work have made that impossible. But we have done something, not least to help defeat a "pro-choice" motion in the students' union.

Of course, my friends might have seen me again during the debate and the vote, but I'm less worried now about what other people might think. If I'm going to Mass I'm even willing to tell my friends where I am going. None of them seems all that bothered. Sometimes I even discover that one of them is a Catholic. People are more open to religion than we give them credit for.

There's obviously a link between my pro-life witness and my faith. Perhaps the prayer vigil and the debate have helped me to be more open about going to Mass. Or perhaps this openness about my faith has enabled me to take a few more risks with pro-life activity. It's not possible to take a step in one area of your life without it affecting everything else as well.

Kabron Henry, postgraduate student in Economics at the University of Manchester about both God and humanity. By going to the Church with our questions, we have found a great *love and compassion for every person*, with social teachings that give practical expression to Jesus' teaching in the Gospels. We have come to understand that what the Church has to say about sexuality and family planning, for example, is the wisest, most beautiful, most human and most liberating advice we have found anywhere.

We might also be challenged at university by people who hold different beliefs from ourselves. Mary, the Mother of Our Lord, for instance, will probably be a bone of contention with some other Christians. Rather than ignoring these beliefs, we can take the opportunity to explore our own faith. For instance, as Catholics we believe that Mary adopted us all as her spiritual children at the foot of the Cross when she received as her son the beloved disciple (see *John* 19:26). This is not some esoteric belief that is of little relevance to our lives.

We can actually gain personal experience of Mary as our spiritual mother. Mary seeks only to bring us all nearer to God, and we can always turn to her for help. Hopefully, we will not do so only in emergencies!

We are also likely to encounter different beliefs through friendships with students from other religions, including Jews, Muslims and Hindus. There is a great richness to the many religious traditions in our world. We have an opportunity to discover the reverence that other religions give to their sacred texts, the richness of their culture and moral life, their faithfulness to regular prayer, or the depth of their meditation[4]. In return, we can share our own faith with students from other religions, gaining greater insight into our own beliefs in the process.

If we are to love God with all our hearts, with all our souls and with all our strength, we need to use the gift of intellect that he has given us; doing so will both complement and reinforce our prayer. *The Catechism of the Catholic Church* has been an amazing resource for us, as have many other Church documents, especially the writings of Pope John Paul II.

The lives of the saints, too, have inspired us and helped us to realise that God calls us all to be saints. St Thérèse of Lisieux, in particular, reminds us that ordinary things – the service of our work, a brief moment of prayer for one in need, a small kindness which we would rather not perform – take on extraordinary value if we strive to put God in the first place in our lives and do everything not for ourselves but for him.[5]

Sharing the revelation

Once we have begun to open ourselves to God by praying and exploring our faith, we will soon feel compelled to share this revelation with others. Our "telling" will sometimes be with words. We will of course be asked to explain our faith, both by those who are keen to hear about it and by those who seek to criticise it; the more we pray and study our faith, the more we will be able to do this. But we should never underestimate the power of the witness we give when we make time for God and allow him to shape our choices and decisions.

We must also do what we can to help people experience love by meeting their material needs. Few in history have exemplified active love inspired by faith better than Mother Teresa: her love for God was the source of her love for the poor. We will find many opportunities to form friendships with other Catholics who want to put the Gospel into practice, and with those who share a commitment to helping to feed or shelter the homeless, caring for the elderly or the sick, and campaigning for respect for human rights. Pro-life witness – upholding the most fundamental of our human rights and declaring the God-given value of every life from conception until natural death – is quite literally a vital issue for young people today. Kabron in his *Student View* (see page 43) describes how his Catholic faith led him to this form of witness.

Gathered together

We were not made to function independently of other people; God has created us to live in communion with others. For all their e-mails and text

---

STUDENT VIEW: Starting a group at University

When I arrived at the Freshers' Fair I looked out for the Catholic Society stall. There wasn't one. Enquiring at the university's chaplaincy centre, I found out about the local Catholic church. The priests at the parish church seemed pleased to be asked by a young person about what was available, but disappointed to have to answer that my age group was not catered for. In many respects this was not a problem for me – I could still attend the sacraments and pray the Rosary.

However, after a few terms it became clear to me that I needed the support of other young Catholics, and one of the local priests suggested some people for me to contact. Fortunately someone was willing to get involved. We soon got talking over a few pints and several games of pool, and realised that our needs were those of Catholics in both the university and the town.

Reaching others like ourselves was a trial, but we put notices in newsletters, posters in porches, sent out an "all student" e-mail and actively recruited people after Masses. We arranged a date for students and young people of the town to meet and discuss their needs and requests. The meeting led to a small group of us agreeing to meet each week.

Every Sunday evening we began to pray the Rosary together and to discuss what we hoped to achieve. There was plenty of emphasis on prayer, participation in the mass, education and socialising, with everyone contributing to the running of the group. Each week we gathered together the prayer intentions of the group. It was a wonderful way of meeting each others' needs and strengthening our Faith. We also now obtain good material on the Faith from a catalogue company called St Anthony Communications[6] and we arranged for a series of talks to be given in the parish by the Faith Movement[7].

Numbers increased as the group became more active in the parish, and with greater numbers came more ideas and assistance. The group ran well and continues to do so, even after the initial members have long since finished their courses.

James Leatherland, a recent Graduate from the University of Luton messages, so many people today feel isolated and unloved. The word "church" means "gathered together" and there are many communities and groups where firstly we can pray, but also simply spend time with others who share our faith.

The first of these communities will be the university chaplaincy, Catholic society or parish, but there are many others. Thousands of young Catholics around the world – ourselves definitely included – have benefitted greatly from the work of Youth 2000 [8], a movement run by young people for young people, which particularly promotes devotion to Jesus in the Eucharist. As well as helping us to develop our prayer lives, it has given us wonderful friends who have the same ideals and goals, and who inspire us and try to help us to see God's ways in all things.

However, if little or nothing at all seems to be going on at your own university then why not start something up? This was the approach that James took in Luton, as he describes on the previous page. You might also want to look at an article on the website that is associated with this Guide – Fr Patrick Burke takes a look at what a university Catholic society is actually for, and how you might go about realising this in practice. [9]

Do not be afraid !

God is interested in every part of our life, and he has a unique plan for each one of us. Our whole lives should reflect God's unending love: our prayers, our work, our words, our friendships, our smile – our everything! We simply have to try to allow God to be at work in us, and through us, to transform the world. As the Second Vatican Council so eloquently announced and as the Pope reminds us, we are all – regardless of who or where we are – called to holiness:

> "Young people of every continent, do not be afraid to be the saints of the new millennium!" [10]

Notes

[1] Pre-World Youth Day gathering, St Peter's Square, Rome, 5th April 2001.

[2] Funeral Mass: Eucharistic Prayer III.

[3] Student LifeNet acts as an umbrella group for university pro-life societies. See p. 104.

[4] And yet, as Christians, we still recognise that we find the fullness of our religious life in Christ, who is the Way, the Truth and the Life (see Second Vatican Council, *Nostra Aetate*, 2).

[5] St Thérèse of Lisieux died at the age of just 24, but has left a wonderful autobiography entitled *Story of a Soul*, available in many editions. See www.ewtn. com/ therese/therese.htm for more information.

[6] See p. 103 for details.

[7] See p. 100 for details.

[8] For details on Youth 2000, see p. 101.

[9] See www.catholicstudent.net

[10] Pope John Paul II, Message on the Occasion of the XVth World Youth Day.

LOOKING TO THE FUTURE
Peter Kahn

You walk into a careers fair and see one stall after another – each one offers you a fast track into management. After several years with little cash to spend and with mounting debts, you have the opportunity to get your hands on some of the extra £400,000 that (they say) a degree can get you over your lifetime. There is the car that you have always dreamed of driving, and a foreign holiday might not go amiss. This after all is the kind of life that our society prizes, and it certainly is pleasant when people around think of you as a success – but is this all there is to life?

Dropping out of the comfort zone

For one thing, not everyone makes it to this prosperous existence quite so easily. While I was still studying, I had to face a chronic illness that lasted for six years. Imagine being unable to brush your teeth

In at the deep end . . .

because the noise it makes is too loud! My earning power was minimal for the whole of this period. Or imagine that a promotion that you've been seeking for several years is not given to you, but to someone else whom you feel is less deserving, and you suspect that it was because of your sex or your race. However much we might decry it and seek to effect change, injustice is still a part of our world. If we build our lives around success then at some point we are sure to be brought down to earth, even if it only becomes apparent at the end of our life.

Give yourself away

What else, then, can we build our lives on if a large salary is not an adequate foundation? There are of course plenty of alternatives. Buddha was convinced that the goal was to extinguish every desire so that the self can be absorbed into the infinite – Nirvana. The modern approach is the exact opposite to Buddha's view: fan your desires into flames, whether for sex, alcohol, food or prestige. The only difficulty, as Buddha realised long ago, is that indulging one desire after the next hardly leads to fulfilment . . .

Fortunately, though, God has given us an answer. In fact, he came down to earth to let us know. And what did Jesus have to say when he arrived? – Give yourself away. Jesus brought the message that absolutely everything we do should be done with an eye to serving both God and others. He

GRADUATE VIEW: A move into consultancy

I fell into my initial career almost by accident – it certainly wasn't planned out far ahead. I'd been looking around for a Masters degree to go into and I'd always had an interest in public transport, so taking a course in transport planning seemed a good idea. Then, when I was exploring sponsors for a possible PhD, I was approached unofficially to see if I was interested in a job instead. So I ended up with London Transport, in Central Planning.

I soon got involved in the early stages of a large project for electronic information displays on bus stops in London, "Countdown". The system tells you how many minutes you are likely to have to wait before the next bus, based on the current traffic situation. I felt strongly about going into a service industry that affects people in their everyday lives. The project helped those who don't have enough wealth to own a car. It made their lives easier. I even received a trickle of letters from people saying how it had helped to change their lives.

During that project, though, I became more interested in general project management; this prompted a move into management consultancy. The role of project manager is to get things done. The approach I take is to encourage and call people on, rather than to use brute force, as many managers do. I try to treat people with respect, seeing this as giving an implicitly Christian example in my work. People have commented that they feel valued and would like to follow a similar approach in their own work.

The nature of consultancy work does, however, make the work-life balance a difficult one to get right. In the first management consultancy that I worked for, I had to do a fair amount of travel abroad, often for long stretches. My wife and I, however, felt that it was getting too much. I managed to find a consultancy that only takes work in or around London. This was a key reason why I joined them. We also decided to live relatively near in to London, rather than further out, so that long journeys were kept to a minimum. The work is demanding and there is relatively little opportunity for life beyond immediate family, but it definitely brings its own reward with it.

Stephen Balogh, a Management Consultant

asked us to make a sincere gift of ourselves and our talents to others. This after all was what Jesus did; he always put others first, even at the cost of his own life.

You will find that when you give yourself away, God gives you back far more in return. This might seem impossible, but not only did Jesus tell us how to find fulfilment, he also made it possible. This chapter explores the practical implications of all of this, and we will look at some options that are not on offer in a careers fair.

What is the meaning of this city?

Your most immediate concern, though, is likely to be the job you will get after university. You might think that there is no need to bother about love when it comes to a job, but, even if you choose a career that is lucrative, the money can hardly be the driving factor in your choice. After all, love of God and love of money are in fact mutually exclusive.

The aim instead should be to choose an option that will enable you to serve others, whether family, friends, those in need or people in society more widely. Careers in the public sector, for example, often fall into this category. This, of course, is not an essential feature, but we can easily deceive ourselves into thinking that we will serve people whatever the job, when the reality is in fact very different. Indeed, some careers seem to positively attract people who are out for themselves and you can only too easily be swept along.

Work also impacts on the rest of your life, and it's often here that the choices you face are the clearest. Time, for instance, is likely to be critical. After all, some jobs seem to require you to be at the office almost all your waking hours. You do need some space in your life for family and friends, for God, and perhaps for voluntary work. You need time to raise a family or even to talk to an elderly neighbour. Where you work also matters. Careers that demand frequent moves need to be chosen

GRADUATE VIEW: Letting God in

I look back in wonder on those last six months at university. It was a frenzied time of exams, job interviews, being "stressed out" – and yet there were good laughs, and there was hope. Hope for the future. All around me, classmates were getting interviews for jobs that paid well, jobs that offered excellent prospects of promotion, jobs that offered security … and yet I wasn't thinking along those lines at all. I was thinking of religious life.

It was a notion that had been with me, on and off, for years, and now that I was finishing my studies, it was decision time. Given the environment I was in, I could well have felt alienated and kept my own thoughts for the future a secret. But nothing could have been further from the reality: since my first year I had gone to Mass every day at the Catholic chaplaincy and there, not surprisingly, I met like-minded people who became an enormous support to me, and I to them. Going to Mass with these friends and having lunch with them afterwards were key features of my time at university, not only because they lent me a true perspective on things when life was becoming too hectic, but also because, regardless of whims and fancies, my centre of gravity was becoming more and more firmly rooted in Christ.

My desire to be a Sister had not been quelled by the temptations and pressures that so often accompany university life – rather the notion of my teenage years was maturing even as I was, and I experienced a certainty and a peace that somehow shielded me from the stress experienced by those around me. With my whole life and new horizons ahead of me, I freely and joyfully made the decision to become a Sister of the Gospel of Life[1]. We are an entirely new religious community that engages in pro-life work.

In the light of the will of God, the Sacraments, and the grace of excellent friendships, the question is not one of wealth, promotion, or worldly ambition. Ask yourself the harder question: what does God want me to do? How will I be personally fulfilled? Who will be at the centre of my life? Out of my friends at the chaplaincy, three went on to seminary and one is a deeply committed member of a lay apostolate. God is at work in all of us, but you have to be open. You have to let Him in.

Sr Andrea Fraile, graduate in Philosophy and Hispanic Studies from Glasgow University with care, as friendships cannot regularly be traded in without some cost; proximity to family and friends is relevant. Stephen, a management consultant, explores on page 48 how he has faced some of these issues.

The reality is that the choices you make lead to different lives. The poet T S Eliot in *Choruses from 'The Rock'* captures this contrast between a life that is centred on work and money, and a life that is centred on love:

> When the Stranger says:
>> "What is the meaning of this city?
> Do you huddle close together
>> because you love each other?"
> What will you answer? "We all dwell together
> To make money from each other"? or
>> "This is a community"?
> And the Stranger will depart
>> and return to the desert.
> O my soul, be prepared for
>> the coming of the Stranger,
> Be prepared for him
>> who knows how to ask questions.

The whole of life

Work is, evidently, not the only way to give yourself away. Indeed, the whole of life needs to be given over to loving others, and that includes our sexuality. The Church recognises that we give ourselves completely both in marriage and when taking a vow of celibacy. The single life also offers plenty of scope to love and serve others. Everyone is single for at least a while, and some people will be called by God to remain so for the whole of their lives. However, this giving to others is not intrinsically bound up with the single life in quite the same way – you need to build it in more deliberately, employing your freedom generously.

There are so many factors that make a married relationship such an opportunity for love. The marriage vows themselves actually constitute a mutual giving to each other. After all, the couple pledge to share absolutely everything for the rest of their lives. Consider the intimacy, stability, common life, sexual bonding and children that find their place in marriage – even one's fertility is taken up in this giving. What could be more romantic than two people who love each other this deeply?

In the case of priests, monks, nuns and other religious brothers and sisters, the giving is more directly to God. As well as taking a vow of celibacy, they all promise obedience to someone else. In addition, religious give away everything they own. Leaving behind all your possessions may strike you as odd, but at least part of this feeling stems from our relative unfamiliarity with the lives of people who have done this. So take a look at the testimony of Sr Andrea on the previous page. But if you really want to understand how this life makes love possible, you need to taste it; spend some time at a monastery or convent, simply with a view to finding out what the religious life is like.[2]

Can you pick a vocation off the shelf?

The call to love and service in our work and our lives still leaves open so many options: several jobs could fit the bill; there might be more than one person you would consider marrying; religious orders differ from each other immensely; and there are plenty of ways to spend your life fulfilled and happy as a single person. Fortunately, God not only calls us to love, he also calls us to a particular expression of this love – our "vocation" is the word traditionally used for this call.

Still, it's not always quite so easy to listen to what God has to say. God speaks in the circumstances of our lives, and in a pull on our hearts and minds rather than in a booming voice. This means that God's voice is easily drowned out by the many clamours around us, perhaps from the media or our friends. So how do you put yourself in a position where you might hear God's call? The simple answer is that you need to allow God into your life. One way to do this is to draw on the contents of this Guide. The chapter on faith, for instance, provides plenty of encouragement to make space for God in your life. Ideas in a guidebook, however, are not enough. We also need the support of other people.

So take up the opportunities that your chaplaincy, Catholic society, or local parish offer you, and use this Guide to help you get in touch. Each chapter in the first part of this Guide has presented you with practical ways to live out your faith during this new time of change in your life; and the second part which now follows provides you with the details of a wide variety of organisations. So make the most of these opportunities to enrich your life and the lives of others: for the future of the Church and of our society is yours to shape. Go for it!

Notes
[1] For details of the Sisters of the Gospel of Life, see the entry for Cardinal Winning's Pro-Life Initiative on p. 105.
[2] See also the National Office for Vocations, p. 103.

Part II: Listings

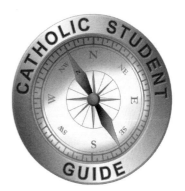

Please note that details concerning the organisations listed in this Guide are subject to change. For instance, the Catholic chaplains to any given institution do change periodically; however, the location of a chaplaincy is much more likely to be constant. Personal e-mail addresses of chaplains, in particular, are therefore more likely to change than the address of a chaplaincy.

Where accommodation is referred to, details are only provided where the provision is organised on an explicitly Catholic basis.

We welcome your comments, corrections or additional material for inclusion in future editions, which can be sent to catholicstudent@hotmail.com or to the editor, c/o the publishers (for address, see page 2). New editions will normally appear biannually. Selected additional materials may be posted on the associated website, www.catholicstudent.net.

– Peter Kahn
Editor

Regional Listings

Greater London: Chaplaincies

Brunel University

Chigwell Convent, 803 Chigwell Road, Woodford Bridge, Essex IG8 8AU

Contact: Sr Patricia Collins SSHJM, Chaplain

Tel: 020 8506 0329
E-mail: shjmpatricia@aol.com

Details: A bungalow building beside Gaskill Buildings, opposite Flemming Hall. Usually open between 9am to 5pm weekdays.

The chaplaincy is located at 'The Meeting House on the Uxbridge Campus and operates ecumenically with students of other faiths. The ecumenical chaplaincy defines itself as 'a spiritual and pastoral resource for the University Community'. The Meeting House is welcoming and supportive. Information is provided about local churches and we have a small library where relevant faith journals and newspapers are available. There is a quiet room for prayer, silence, or relaxation, self-catering facilities and a large room which can be hired.

Central London Universities Catholic Chaplaincy

(Birkbeck College, City University, Courtauld Institute, Institute of Education, King's College London, London Metropolitan University (City Campus), London School of Economics, Medical Schools, Royal Academy of Dramatic Arts, Royal Academy of Music, School of African and Oriental Studies, School of Hygiene and Tropical Medicine, School of Latin American Studies, School of Pharmacy, School of Slavonic and Eastern European Studies, University College London, University of Westminster)

Newman House,
111 Gower Street,
London WC1E 6AR
www.universitycatholic.net

Contact: Rev Peter Wilson, Rev Tim Calvert OP and Sr Patricia Collins SSHJM, Chaplains

Tel: 020 7387 6370
E-mail: enquiries@universitycatholic.net

Details: Central london, opposite UCL. Nearest tube: Euston Square, Goodge Street, Warren Street. Chapel, library, meeting rooms, bar.

Central Catholic Chaplaincy to the universities of London. Daily Mass Mon–Fri at 5.30pm, Sat 9am. Sunday Mass at 10.30am and 7.30pm. Exposition of the Blessed Sacrament and morning prayer, Mon–Fri, 8–8.30am; Rosary, Tuesdays 5.10pm; night prayer and Benediction, Wednesday 10pm. Talks and conferences on the Catholic Faith; faith sharing and prayer groups facilitated by the chaplains; confession on call; Chaplains freely available. Residential retreats arranged and social outreach activities organised. Student bar providing social events, bar suppers and informative talks. Chaplaincy and Catholic Society support offered in individual Colleges.

Accommodation: 63 individual rooms with washbasin and refrigerator, centrally heated, showers and bathrooms on every floor, self-service breakfast provided.

Three kitchens available for self-catering, together with storage space. Launderette and telephones. TV room and library.

Digby Stuart College, University of Surrey

www.roehampton.ac.uk/chaplaincy/

Details: Mass is celebrated each day of the week in the College. As well as the Main Chapel, there is a Sacred Heart Chapel and Prayer Room. The Chaplaincy is located behind the Chapel. For further details of the provision for Catholic chaplaincy, please see the above webpage or approach the College.

University of East London

Details: For details of the provision for Catholic chaplaincy, please approach the University.

University of Greenwich

Department of Student Affairs, University of Greenwich, Maritime Greenwich Campus, Old Royal Naval College, Park Row, London SE10 9LS
www.gre.ac.uk/students/services/re/

Contact: Ms Gabrielle Power BMus (Hons) PGCE, Chaplain

Tel: 020 8331 8151 / 7868
E-mail: G.Power@gre.ac.uk

Details: Chaplains are located within the Department of Student Affairs. There is a Chaplaincy office at Avery Hill campus, and the Chaplain uses Student Affairs facilities at Maritime Greenwich. See website for further details.

The RC Chaplaincy at the University of Greenwich works ecumenically with colleagues from other denominations to provide pastoral and spiritual support, discussions, reflection and opportunities for students to meet and socialise together. There is Mass provided on campus for Holy Days in the grand setting of the Old Royal Naval College Chapel. Other prayers and services are provided throughout the year. There is an active discussion and social group called 'Questioning Christians' which meets weekly to discuss interesting and controversial topics. Chaplains are also available to support students in all aspects of their life at University. They are often involved in University activities such as the University Choir. Currently the Chaplains are located within the Dept of Student Affairs at Maritime Greenwich Campus. Avery Hill campus has a Chaplaincy office. Gabrielle Power is a married lay woman employed by the Catholic Church to work with students and staff at the University of Greenwich. She is part of the South London Catholic Chaplaincy team, and some activities such as weekly Mass, theatre trips, talks, parties, etc. are organised jointly by the team. Gabrielle has close links with many of the parishes in the area and can help you find out where to go to Mass. Students are also encouraged to come to the 5pm Mass at the Chaplaincy, 56 Amersham Road, New Cross, which is followed by refreshments, usually a shared meal.

Guy's and Thomas's Medical Schools at King's College, and St George's Medical School

GKT Chaplaincy at King's College, The Mezzanine, Henriette Raphael Building, King's College, Guy's Campus, London Bridge, London SE1
www.kcl.ac.uk/chaplaincy

Contact: Awaiting appointment

Tel: 020 7848 6940

Details: The Chaplaincy, known as 'The Mezzanine' consists of Chaplaincy office and Quiet Room with tea- and Coffee-making facilities. Located between the first and second floors of Henriette Raphael Building, Guy's Campus, King's College.

The Catholic chaplain is part of the ecumenical chaplaincy team. Together they have a programme which includes video nights, social events and parties, at the local Catholic chaplaincy flat. There is weekly evening prayer and regular social events such as beginning- and end-of-term and seasonal parties (e.g. Christmas, Pancake party, BBQs, etc). Regular Masses and services, (such as the popular candle-lit Carol Service) are held in Guy's chapel. Theatre trips and other social events take place throughout the year. Volunteering at Melior Street, 5–6pm week-nights: there is a Volunteer soup kitchen project at local Catholic Church 'Our Lady of La Salette & St Joseph', Melior Street, providing food for the homeless. Contact Rev James Buxton through the chaplaincy office for further details. The chaplaincy office is well staffed and chaplains are available for prayer, support and advice.

Heythrop College

Heythrop College, University of London, 23 Kensington Gardens, London W8 5HQ
www.heythrop.ac.uk

Contact: Bernie Devine, Chaplain

Tel: 020 7795 6600 / 4215

E-mail: b.devine@heythrop.ac.uk

Details: In a college such as Heythrop, all members of staff care for the welfare of the students. In addition, the College offers a confidential service of pastoral support through the Chaplaincy/Student Support Service. Those who belong to other faith groups and those with no specific faith affiliation are equally the concern of the Chaplain who is appointed to be of service to all students, offering welcome, availability, friendship and appropriate forms of pastoral care.

Imperial College London, Royal College of Art, Royal College of Music

More House, 53 Cromwell Road, London SW7 2EH

Contact: Rev Geoff Wheaton SJ, Chaplain

Tel: 020 7584 2040

E-mail: rcchaplainmore@aol.com

Details: Imperial College Chaplaincy is in Beit Quad, adjacent to Students' Union. Facilities include office, meeting room, tea & coffee facilities, library.

The Chaplaincy of Imperial College serves all three colleges and is staffed Mon to Fri from 9am to 5pm. Thursday Mass in Imperial College at 1pm. Mass is held Mon, Tues 8pm, and Wed, Fri 7.50am at More House. Discussion and prayer groups at both Imperial College and More House. All Catholic students are invited to use the extensive facilities at More House including TV room, bar, library and chapel.

Accommodation: More House is a residence for 75–80 students, and is run by the Canonesses of St Augustine. (See entry for More House below.)

Kingston University

102 Maple Road, Kingston-upon-Thames, Surrey KT6 4AL
www.rc.net/southwark/straphael/index.htm

Contact: Rev Vincent Flynn, Chaplain

Tel: 020 8399 1574

Details: St Raphael's Catholic Church (Portsmouth Road, Kingston upon Thames). Located very near the Penwyn Road site, this beautiful Italianate traditional church is a haven for the weary soul in need of spiritual refreshment. Mass, confessions, Rosary, Benediction, etc. Fr Vincent is very approachable, easy-going and a good listener.

The Chaplaincy is just being renewed, so please make contact and be part of the great Catholic revival in Kingston.

London Metropolitan University, North Campus

The Chaplaincy, London Metropolitan University, 166–220 Holloway Road, London N7 8DB

Contact: Sr Patricia Collins SSHJM, Chaplain

Tel: 020 7133 2813
E-mail: shjmpatricia@aol.com

Details: Chaplaincy is in Tower Building, 1st floor. A large room with quiet room inset. All doubles up as office of local C of E dean, who is full-time. Tea/coffee-making facilities and cassette recorder available.

Hospitality on a drop-in, phone or e-mail basis; usually individual. Tea/coffee/chat. Quiet room available, small library of Christian/Catholic books. Occasional Mass, Bible study and prayer on a request basis.

Accommodation: We put up adverts and recommend accommodation. Unfortunately the chaplaincy has no accommodation to offer.

Queen Mary and Westfield College

Details: The ecumenical Chaplaincy Centre is located near the main entrance to the campus on Mile End Road. Please approach the College for details of the provision for Catholic chaplaincy.

Roehampton, University of Surrey

www.roehampton.ac.uk/chaplaincy/

Details: Roehampton is an ecumenical institution, with comprehensive Chaplaincy provision. The Chaplains work together to support students across the whole institution. For details of the provision for Catholic chaplaincy, please approach the institution.

Royal Holloway, University of London

www.rhul.ac.uk/chaplaincy/chaplains.html

Details: For details of the Catholic Chaplaincy provision, please approach the College. The office of the Catholic Chaplain to the College is on the first floor of Founder's West.

South London Universities Catholic Chaplaincy

(Goldsmiths College, Laban School of Dance, University of Greenwich, South Bank University, Trinity College of Music)

South London Universities Catholic Chaplaincy, 56 Amersham Road, New Cross, London SE14 6QE

Contact: Awaiting appointment

Tel: 020 8692 6931
E-mail: G.Power@gre.ac.uk

Details: The Chaplaincy Building, 56 Amersham Road, is situated within 5 minutes' walk from Goldsmiths College, just off Lewisham Way (first house on the left). It has a chapel, small library, kitchen and dining room, a student lounge, and accommodation for the Goldsmiths Chaplain and two students. The Chaplaincy is just over five minutes' walk from New Cross Station and 10–15 minutes from New Cross Gate. Both provide good links into Central London. From Greenwich, the 177 bus takes you to New Cross station and Goldsmiths College. The Goldsmiths Chaplain also uses the newly opened Chaplaincy Centre (ecumenical) at Goldsmiths College, under the arch at the side of the main building. The weekly Christian Aid soup/sandwiches lunch takes place there on Tuesday lunchtime.

The chaplaincy is for all South London higher education students, whatever institution they attend. The chaplaincy provides a 5pm Sunday Chaplaincy Mass during term time followed by refreshments/meals, social time and Mass on Holy Days (5.30pm). There is a varied programme on offer including talks, prayers, retreats and theatre trips, open to all students, not to mention seasonal parties, BBQs, etc. The chaplains plan this as a team, whilst also working ecumenically within the institutions they serve. Chaplains are available to talk in confidence both in their main institution and at the chaplaincy (by appointment or drop in). Confessions are arranged on request, usually before the Sunday Mass. We hope we can help you make the most of your experience at University. Two new appointments are being made to the chaplaincy team in Summer 2003. To contact the newly appointed team members, please use the above e-mail address.

St Mary's College

St. Mary's College, Waldegrave Road, Twickenham, Middlesex TW1 4SX
www.smuc.ac.uk

Contact: Rev Gerard Devlin, College Chaplain

Tel: 020 8240 4006
E-mail: devling@smuc.ac.uk

Details: Chapel and chaplaincy at heart of campus.

Chaplaincy provides a focus for the community life of this Catholic College and offers support for individual students and staff. It also works to foster a nurturing environment at the college, reflecting a real concern for the development and well-being of the whole person. Communal worship is important to the life of the college. Daily Mass, Sacrament of Reconciliation on request, Multi-faith Prayer Room and a weekly chaplaincy newsletter. Groups and Activities include liturgical ministries, social events, choir, music group, music days, RCIA, sacramental preparation, prayer journey retreats, a pastoral council, Lenten and Easter retreats, ecumenical prayer group, Taizé evenings, Simms Lourdes HCPT, Christian Union, Pastoral Theology study days and lectures, justice and peace ministry, choir festival and carol singing. (See also the entry for St Mary's College under 'Catholic Education'.)

Accommodation: Accommodation is available from the College.

Greater London: Organisations

Acton Homeless Concern

1 Berrymead Gardens, Acton, London W3 8AA

Contact: Sr Aileen Kennedy, Director

Tel: 020 8992 5768

Details: Two drop-in centres for homeless people. Free hot lunch at midday, tea and sandwiches from 4–8pm. Free clothes, showers, haircuts. Visiting doctor, chiropodist, optician, benefits officer and rough sleepers advisor. Opportunity for students to do voluntary work and help those less fortunate.

Ashwell House

Shepherdess Walk, London N1 7NA
www.ashwell.dircon.co.uk

Contact: Sam Pleasants, Warden

Tel: 020 7490 5021
E-mail: ashwelloffice@btconnect.com

Details: Situated in the heart of London, within easy reach of many London University colleges. With the provision of excellent study conditions, Ashwell offers female students a warm and supportive family atmosphere, which is also intellectually stimulating. Fully catered, with clean, individual study rooms. Annual programme of talks by guest speakers, conferences and concerts. Linked with social and welfare projects offering voluntary work opportunities both at home and abroad during term time and holiday period. Spiritual activities are entrusted to Opus Dei, a prelature of the Catholic Church. Daily Mass, theology classes, philosophy seminars given by Chaplain. Open to people of all faiths and none.

Break open the word (18+)

St Patrick's Roman Catholic Church, Waterloo, London

Contact: Ms Karen North

Tel: 020 8672 7684
E-mail: knorth@cectootingbec.org.uk

Details: Break open the word (18+) provides an opportunity for young people to come together to reflect on the Word of God and share the Eucharist, followed by social time: 7pm Mass followed by social time, first Thursday of the month. This is an initiative of Southwark Catholic Youth Service and Diocesan Christian Education Centre. This is a local initiative appropriate to students and organised by a former chaplain.

Catholic Children's Society (Westminster)

73 St Charles Square, London W10 6EJ
www.cathchild.org.uk

Contact: Rosemary Keenan, Deputy Director

Tel: 020 8969 5305
E-mail: rosemaryk@cathchild.org.uk

Details: Opportunities for voluntary work. Opportunities for placements. Adoption/family placement service.

Communion and Liberation

www.clonline.org.uk

Tel: 0799 0543866
E-mail: cl_uk@onetel.net.uk

Details: Weekly meetings are held in London where we help each other to share and judge our lives in the light of the encounter with Christ. During the year, national retreats and holidays are organised, with students from universities all around the UK. Please refer to our entry under 'New Movements and Evangelisation' for further information.

Elmore Study Centre

8 Orme Court, London W2 4RL

Contact: Mr Jack Valero

Tel: 020 7243 9411

Details: Elmore is a centre for men students seeking to get more out of their university life than just beer and books. The centre encourages serious study, and has a small library available for student use with an excellent study atmosphere, but it also organises cultural, sporting, spiritual and social service activities. Elmore Study Centre is a place to meet students from other universities and countries in an informal, family environment. For those who wish, talks and conferences on the Catholic faith and other formational activities are organised, open also to non-Catholics. A chaplain is available for individual spiritual guidance. Spiritual activities are run by Opus Dei, a personal prelature of the Church.

Focolare Movement

62 Kings Avenue, London SW4 8BH
www.focolare.org

Contact: Pat Whitney, Communications Assistant

Tel: 020 8671 8355

E-mail: pat@focolare.demon.co.uk

Details: Focolare is an international movement started by Chiara Lubich in Trent, Italy, in 1943. Its principal aim is to contribute to the fulfilment of Jesus' prayer, "May they all be one". It is at the service of dialogue within and between churches, with people of different faiths, and with those who want to work for peace and unity in all spheres of society. The young people's section, known as Youth for a United World, organises activities in London, as well as elsewhere.

Franciscan Friars of the Renewal

St Fidelis Friary, Killip Close,
Canning Town, London E16 1LX
www.franciscanfriars.com

Contact: Br John-Paul, Local Servant

Tel: 020 7474 0766

Details: Opportunities to shelter the homeless, volunteering at boys' basketball clubs, or local home visits with families.

Spiritual opportunities include 1st Saturday Associates gathering, Lectio Divina evenings and pro-life vigils.

Goodenough College

Goodenough College, Mecklenburgh Square, London WC1N 2AB
jdawer.homestead.com/come.html

Contact: Rev John Dawer SVD, Chaplain

Tel: 020 7837 4147
E-mail: jdawer@hotmail.com

Details: Goodenough College is an international hall of residence for postgraduates. It houses 600 students (single and with families). It is is open to all faiths. Usually, per year, around 70 catholics get the opportunity to stay. Catholic Chaplaincy is part of this college. Sunday Mass at 10am. Weekly prayer meeting on Thursdays at 8:30 pm, Confessions by appointment, Personal guidance by appointment, Alpha courses, House retreats, Past talks, Seminars. Accommodation available for students if applied for well in advance. The College also offers a chapel, library, four meeting rooms, a gym/swimming pool, a garden/jogging park, tennis ground.

Koinonia

31 Lynton Rd, Acton, London W3 9HL
www.koinonia.co.uk

Contact: Nico Angleys, Director

Tel: 07799 067470
E-mail: info@koinonia.co.uk

Details: Koinonia exists for students in Central London to help them discover the call of God in their lives and to provide environments which allow them to respond to the challenge of that call. Koinonia meets weekly to pray and worship together. Some students choose to live in households for the year to experience deeper fellowship and discipleship together. Koinonia also offers opportunities to share life with Christians from other churches and ecclesial communities.

London Catholic Worker

c/o Angela Broome, 14 Deal Street,
London E1 5AH
www.geocities.com/londoncatholicworker

Contact: Mr Scott Albrecht

Tel: 07941 773542   **E-mail:** londoncatholicworker@yahoo.co.uk

Details: This is a faith-based group. The group practises works of mercy, resistance to organised violence (militarism) and hospitality. It offers a place to pray, reflect and act together and in solidarity with those who suffer injustice.

Maria Assumpta Centre

23 Kensington Square, London W8 5HN

Contact: Ms Helen Granger, Head of Student Services

Tel: 020 7361 4700   **E-mail:** studentservices@mariaassumpta.freeserve.co.uk

Details: A residence for 115 women students, 18–30, in full-time education. There is a mix of nationalities, cultures, faiths, academic subjects and levels of study. This is intended to build bonds of friendship, understanding and co-operation. There is a chapel on the campus, Sunday Mass and weekday lunchtime Mass in term-time.

More House

53 Cromwell Road, London SW7 2EH

Contact: Sr Francoise Georgeault, Warden

Tel: 020 7584 2040

E-mail: more-house@surf3.net

Details: Accommodation to university students in single and twin-bedded rooms. Breakfast everyday, evening meals Monday to Friday. It has a resident Chaplain, chapel, library, TV room and laundry.

Neocatechumenal Way, London (4 groups)

London E1

Contact: Tony and Sheila Cook

Tel: 020 77901 380

E-mail: cooktony@btinternet.com

London SE15

Contact: Ras and Philippa Thomasen

Tel: 020 7732 1149

E-mail: jrthomasen@yahoo.co.uk

London SW7

Contact: Michael and Dorothy Anderson

Tel: 020 7584 2579

E-mail: michael.anderson@htb.org.uk

London W5

Contact: Peter and Colleen Wallach

Tel: 020 8579 5716

E-mail: peterwallach@lineone.net

Details: The Neocatechumenal Way is an itinerary of Catholic formation which, lived in small communities within the parish, helps people to rediscover and to live the immense riches of their baptism.

After an initial set of teachings on the Catholic faith, those who wish to do so will form and continue as a community which then meets on a regular basis to celebrate together the Liturgy of the Word and the Eucharist, going through various stages similar to those of the 'catechumenate' of the Early Church. The Neocatechumenal Way is governed by a Statute approved by the Holy See.

Netherhall House

Netherhall House, Nutley Terrace, London NW3 5SA
www.nh.netherhall.org.uk

Contact: Mr Peter Brown, Director

Tel: 020 7435 8888

E-mail: director@nh.netherhall.org.uk

Details: Netherhall House attracts students keen to develop fully their personality and potential through conscientious study and participation in extra-curricular activities. It is a hall of residence for men, with easy access to all the colleges of the University of London and most of the capital's higher education institutions. Thus residents can also meet students from other colleges. Each year the hall's 100 students come from an average of 30 countries. Typical Netherhall activities include the weekly guest speaker series with leading figures from the fields of politics, the arts, science and academia. There are numerous sporting opportunities (including football, basketball, squash and mountain biking), organised cultural or outdoor excursions, a monthly chamber music recital series and a yearly hall play, all open to those who want to participate. The hall also organises social service activities in London, an annual voluntary project in Nicaragua and opportunities to teach English on summer camps in England and Spain. The hall is open to people of all faiths and none. The house chaplain celebrates Mass daily in the chapel and runs courses on the Catholic Faith throughout the year. The pastoral care of the hall is entrusted to the Opus Dei

prelature. Accommodation is in centrally heated single study bedrooms, and the hall has a library, computer rooms, an auditorium and indoor and outdoor sports surfaces.

Oasis Prayer Meetings – 'Oases'

S.E.N.T., Sawyers Hall Lane, Brentwood, Essex CM15 9BX
www.oases.org.uk

Contact: Alice Hall and Marianna Baccelliere, Co-ordinators

Tel: 01277 215011

E-mail: info@oases.org.uk

Details: Our vision: 'turning dry ground into springs of water' (Is 41:18b–20) – to refresh, to revive, to make ready!

The Oases are growing communities of young people responding to God's call to radical faith; through this prayer network we are inspiring, equipping and motivating our generation to become the saints of the new millennium! Oasis prayer meetings take place in London, as well as elsewhere. Each Oasis community meets monthly and contains the four core elements; Fellowship, Adoration, Intercession, and Praise and Worship.

The Passage

St Vincent's Centre, Carlisle Place, London SW1P 1NL
www.passage.org.uk

Contact: Sr Ellen Flynn, Director

Tel: 020 7592 1850

E-mail: Ellen@passage.org.uk

Details: The opportunity to work on volunteer placements across the organisation, with the most vulnerable people of our society. We provide hostel and day-centre services to homeless people.

Providence Row Charity

Providence Row Charity, Peter Rigby House, 41 Spelman Street, London E1 5LQ
www.providencerow.org.uk

Contact: Ms Laura Macmillen, Volunteer Programme Co-ordinator

Tel: 020 7422 6392

E-mail: volunteer@providencerow.org.uk

Details: Providence Row Charity – A Christian and Professional Response to Homelessness. Did you know that most people in the UK are only three pay-packets away from being homeless? Founded by a Catholic priest in 1860, Providence Row offers you an amazing hands-on opportunity to help tackle poverty and social exclusion on the borders of the City of London. Whether you help three days a week or once a month, preparing food, supporting vulnerable women, training as a counsellor or helping people find a home, you will mix with a wide range of service users and volunteers, from people sleeping rough to employees in City firms. It's hard work, but you will have training, support, and a lot of fun. Sharing our values of respect, empowerment, justice, compassion and inclusiveness, and working with people of different faiths, this is the chance to put yours into action.

Simon Community

PO Box 1187, London NW5 4HW
www.simoncommunity.org

Contact: Marie Cafferky, Administrator

Tel: 020 7485 6639   **E-mail:** thesimoncommunity@hotmail.com

Details: The Simon Community is a volunteer community, Catholic in foundation, Christian in inspiration, open to people of all faiths and none. Since 1963 we have been living and working as a partnership with on-the-street homeless people in London. Full-time residential and part-time volunteers are always needed. We do street work and soup runs, and run residential houses. We also campaign on issues affecting homeless people.

St George's Cathedral

St George's Cathedral, Lambeth Road, Southwark, London SE1

Tel: 020 7928 5256

E-mail: stgeorges@rc.net

Details: The cathedral church of the Archdiocese of Southwark.

Verbum Dei

Verbum Dei, St. Anne's Church, Underwood Road, Whitechapel, London E1 5AW
www.verbum-dei.co.uk

Contact: Yolande Wilson, Young Adults Communications/Publicity Worker

Tel: 020 7375 3964

E-mail: verbum_dei@hotmail.com

Details: Communities/prayer groups of living faith that seek to pray with the Word of God, live in accordance with the Gospel, and witness our faith in contemporary society. Means offered include: prayer meetings, youth encounters, retreats, talks, schools of evangelisation.

Westminster Cathedral

Metropolitan Cathedral of the Most Precious Blood, Victoria Street and Ambrosden Avenue, London SW1P

Tel: 020 7798 9055

Details: The cathedral church of the Archdiocese of Westminster.

Midlands: Chaplaincies

Aston University

Poveda House, 41 Somerset Road, Birmingham B20 2JE

Contact: Rev Peter J Conley, Chaplain

Tel: 0121 523 2778

E-mail: P.J.Conley@aston.ac.uk

Details: The Catholic Chaplain is based in the Martin Luther King Chaplaincy Centre in the courtyard at the back of Lawrence Tower student residence.

Sunday Mass, 7pm in the Martin Luther King Chaplaincy Centre. Holy Days of Obligation Mass, 1.05pm. Taizé prayers weekly, Bible Reflection group, Social events. Chaplain is available to: help and listen to students and staff; offer confidential support; provide advice on spiritual and ethical matters; and offer opportunities for reflection and worship.

University of Birmingham

Newman House, 29 Harrisons Road, Birmingham B15 3QS
www.bham.ac.uk/chaplaincy

Contact: Rev Stephen Pimlott, Chaplain

Tel: 0121 454 4395

E-mail: s.j.pimlott@bham.ac.uk

Details: The Catholic chaplaincy is called Newman House, and is on Harrisons Road off Somerset Road. It contains a chapel, bar, meeting room, halls and a small library.

There are two Sunday Masses (10.30am and 6.30pm) at Newman House, and Cathsoc holds its meetings after the evening Mass. The morning Mass continues through the vacation. Cathsoc runs a variety of social events with some speakers. Weekly Mass, Rosary and Exposition take place at St Francis Hall behind the Guild of Students. "Life in the

Spirit" Seminars have been a special feature of the last two years. Other events aimed at deepening faith and understanding also take place. RCIA and reception classes as necessary. There are many ecumenical and joint activities including the weekly ecumenical service on Wednesdays and at the "Crosslinks retreat".

Accommodation: For 12 students (self-catering).

University of Central England

Cedd House, 80 Aldridge Road, Perry Barr, Birmingham B42 2PT
www.faith.uce.ac.uk

Contact: Sr Christina McCann MA, Chaplain

E-mail: christina.mccann@uce.ac.uk

Details: The Catholic chaplaincy is in the Coppice Hall of Residence, Wellhead Lane (with chapel, common room and kitchen). The ecumenical chaplaincy is in Baker Building, Students' Services Department (with a large meeting room, kitchen and chaplaincy office).

Worship/prayer; support for International students; counselling; retreats; social activities; free lunch weekly; contact with local churches; inter-cultural activities; pastoral/spiritual care of students; ecumenical prayer weekly; relaxation courses weekly; involved with disabled students.

Accommodation: Cedd House has accommodation for six students.

Coventry University

Chaplaincy, Priory Hall, Priory Street, Coventry CV1 5FB
www.coventry.ac.uk/structur/ss/rel-prov

Contact: Rev Aloysius Bukenya and Sr Mary Deane, Chaplains

Tel: 02476 888038

E-mail: m.deane@coventry.ac.uk
chaplaincy@coventry.ac.uk

Details: The university chaplaincy is located in Priory Hall on the ground floor of G-block. The Catholic chaplaincy is located at 16 Stoney Road.

The chaplaincy provides a space to meet others, information on churches and times of Masses throughout Coventry, voluntary work, events, etc. It is a space to ask for help, chat or just time to think, and also provides free tea and coffee. During the day the chaplains are available at the the chaplaincy and there are various organised activities, both social and spiritual, to take part in. The Catholic chaplaincy is located at 16 Stoney Road; it is a residential block and provides accommodation for students as well as a focus for Catholic students to meet, discuss, or just socialise. During term time, Mass is celebrated on a Sunday evening at 7pm in the chapel.

Accommodation: The Catholic chaplaincy at 16 Stoney Road is a residential house, offering accommodation for six students.

De Montfort University

Chaplaincy/Religious Support,
The Gateway, Leicester LE1 9BH

Contact: Sr M Felix Riley OP, Chaplain

Tel: 0116 250 6389

E-mail: Leicchap@dmu.ac.uk

Details: Located at present in the 'Arts Block', while awaiting the completion of a new 'General Purposes Block' in which the chaplaincy will have a suite of rooms. Sitting and eating areas, a chapel, two offices and a kitchenette.

Serves De Monfort University (Leicester Campus). Sr Riley works among an ecumenical team, receiving good and loyal support from two Catholic priests who alternately celebrate Mass weekly on the campus. These priests are on call for students and staff and are also both university chaplains to the nearby University of Leicester. She works part-time, two full days a week, and is available for any Catholic student or staff member. She also does ecumenical pastoral support where she would see any visitor who came into the Chaplaincy. She takes part in short scripture study groups in the chaplaincy and in talks relating to theology and contemporary issues such as homelessness. On Sundays her students join with the Catholic students from the University of Leicester to meet for the celebration of Mass followed by a social event at a venue between the two Leicester Universities, which is The Old School House, situated next door to Holy Cross Church, Wellington Street. (0116 255 5552, website www.Church.jsite.co.uk/holycross). The two universities have a joint Cathsoc which is also building up its university St Vincent de Paul group.

Derby, University of

www.derby.ac.uk/chaplaincy/index.asp

Details: For details of the provision for Catholic chaplaincy, please approach the University.

Keele University

12 The Village, Keele, Newcastle, Staffordshire ST5 5AR

Contact: Rev P.J. Griffin, Chaplain

Tel: 01782 628352

Details: University chapel on campus on Union Square (Chapels, office, meeting room); Catholic chaplaincy in Keele Village opposite post office (Chaplain's home, Cathsoc venue, social activities).

Mass: Sun and Thurs. Eucharistic Adoration: Tuesday evening. Cathsoc: Thursday evenings.

Instruction/discussion group: Wed lunchtimes. Sunday lunch for students at Catholic chaplaincy. Music group assists at Sunday Mass. Annual retreat and ecumenical services.

Leicester University

Holy Cross Priory, 45 Wellington Street, Leicester LE1 6HW

Contact: Rev Richard J Ounsworth OP and Rev Thomas Crean OP, Chaplains

Tel: 0116 252 1512 **E-mail:** richard.ounsworth@english.op.org thomas.crean.op.org

Details: Holy Cross Priory is in the very heart of the city. Part of the priory building is given over to a common room for students, which has a small built-in kitchen. The Gatehouse is directly across the road from the main academic campus.

Leicester University is served, as far as Catholic Chaplaincy is concerned, by the Dominican Friars (Order of Preachers) based in Holy Cross Priory. There is a Mass in the Parish Hall adjoining the priory especially for students on Sunday evenings at 7.15pm, and a free minibus is provided to the various halls of residence of Leicester University. Students are encouraged to take an active part in the life of the parish, attending if they prefer Masses other than the student Mass: the Sunday 11am Mass (in Latin twice a month). After the Student Mass, refreshments are provided and one of the chaplains is always available for students to take out to the pub. The chaplains are fully involved in the Leicester University Ecumenical Chaplaincy, which is based in The Gatehouse. Mass in said in The Gatehouse chapel at 1.35pm on Wednesdays and Fridays.The Gatehouse is also the usual base for the Catholic Society, which meets on Wednsday evenings for talks, discussions, videos and other events. Many activities are held in common with students and chaplains from De Montfort University.

Lincoln, University of

www.lincoln.ac.uk/studentservices/ Chaplaincy/chap.htm

Details: For details of the provision for Catholic chaplaincy, please approach the University.

Loughborough University

49 Fairmount Drive, Loughborough, Leicestershire LE11 3JR

Contact: Rev Michael Tutcher, Chaplain

Tel: 01509 217013

Details: Chapel in Edward Herbert Building at the centre of the University Campus. Chapel Library, meeting and prayer rooms.

Chaplaincy to Loughborough University and colleges. Facilities: chapel with library and prayer rooms. Masses weekdays, Saturday and Sunday. Retreats, social, intellectual opportunities. Close relationship with town through university worship community. Catholic Chaplaincy involved ecumenically with Chaplaincy team.

Newman College of Higher Education

Newman College of Higher Education, Genners Lane, Bartley Green, Birmingham B32 3NT www.newman.ac.uk

Contact: College Chaplain

Tel: 0121 476 1181

Details: St Mary's Chapel is at the heart of the campus. There is a library of spiritual books in the Prayer Room at the back of the College chapel. There is also a Muslim prayer room located in College.

Mass: on Sunday at 6.30 pm. Mon, Wed, Fri at 12.30 pm. Morning Prayer: offered at 8.45 am each morning. Sacrament of Reconciliation: every Sunday from 6–6.30 pm and on individual request. SVP Society: undertaking voluntary work in Birmingham. Taizé Prayer gatherings: first Tuesday of each month. Soup Lunch: every Wednesday raising money for CAFOD. College Choir: every Tuesday, singing at all College events and participating in Church Colleges Choir Festival. Retreats, opportunities for Bible Study and spiritual growth, programmes for training in ministries, e.g. readers, eucharistic ministers. Newman has a lively interactive Church group in the Christian Union. (See also the entry for Newman College of Higher Education in the 'Catholic Education' section.)

Accommodation: Halls of residence are on campus for around 300 or so students. As a Catholic college, Newman respects and welcomes people of all faiths and none.

Nottingham Trent University

Cathedral House, North Circus Street, Nottingham NG1 5AE

Contact: Rev Christopher Thomas, Chaplain

Tel: 0115 953 9839
E-mail: christopher.thomas@ntu.ac.uk

Details: City site: Dryden Building, Dryden Street, Nottingham.
Clifton site: Student Support Building, Main Campus, Clifton Lane, Nottingham.

Weekly Mass on Thursdays at the City site (Dryden Centre). Students' Sunday Mass at St Barnabas Cathedral at 6pm followed by a social. The Chaplain is normally at the university on Thursdays only, but may be contacted at any time at the Cathedral. The Nottingham Trent University Chaplaincy is a local Ecumenical partnership working within the University to promote the Kingdom of God.

University of Nottingham

www.nottingham.ac.uk/chaplains/

Details: For details of the provision for Catholic chaplaincy, please approach the University. The chaplains' offices are located at the West end of the Portland Building on the main campus.

Staffordshire University

Newman House, 6 Winton Square, Station Road, Stoke-on-Trent ST4 2AD
Contact: Rev Brian Wall SJ
Tel: 01782 844656

University of Warwick

www.warwick.ac.uk/chaplaincy/index1.htm

Details: The ecumenical chaplaincy is located on the Central campus. For details of the provision for Catholic chaplaincy, please approach the University.

University of Wolverhampton

Giffard House, 51 North Street, Wolverhampton WV1 1RJ

Contact: Rev Patrick H Daly, Chaplain

Tel: 01902 423005
E-mail: phdaly@pacelli.fsnet.co.uk

Details: Chaplaincy building, Molineaux Street (next to hall of residence, opposite Asda)

Sunday Masses: 5.30pm (Saturday Vigil); 10:15 am (Family Mass); 6.45pm. Presence in chaplaincy building: weekdays, 2.00-4.00 pm. Student party at Giffard House on 2nd Sunday of every month (or as announced). Individual couselling.

Accommodation: Four student rooms in Giffard House, twelve rooms in house on Paul Rd East. Contact number: 01902 423 005.

Midlands: Organisations

Birmingham Oratory

The Oratory, 141 Hagley Road, Edgbaston, Birmingham B16 8UE
www.birmingham-oratory.org.uk

Contact: Very Rev Paul Chavasse, Superior

Tel: 0121 454 0496

E-mail: oratory@globalnet.co.uk

Details: Three weekday Masses, four on Sundays. Daily confessions. Benediction twice weekly. Brothers of the Little Oratory meet weekly for prayer, talks and socialising. Students sing in the choir, which performs at Solemn Mass on Sunday mornings and Vespers Sunday evenings, plus major feasts. The Fathers are always available for spiritual direction, etc.

Cathedral of St Barnabas

Cathedral of St Barnabas, Derby Road, Nottingham NG1 5AE

Tel: 0115 953 9839

Details: The cathedral church of the Diocese of Nottingham.

Cursillos in Christianity

Clayton House, Newlands Lane, Stoke Row, Henley-on-Thames RG9 5QS
www.cursillo.org.uk

Contact: Mr Stephen Fox, National Secretary

Tel: 01491 681646

E-mail: stephen.fox@cursillo.org.uk

Details: Cursillo is a Catholic movement to form leaders, who grow through prayer, study and action to evangelise others for Christ.

The movement is active in the Diocese of Birmingham and elsewhere. Three-day weekends are run on a Diocesan basis.

Oasis Prayer Meetings – 'Oases'

S.E.N.T., Sawyers Hall Lane, Brentwood, Essex CM15 9BX
www.oases.org.uk

Contact: Alice Hall and Marianna Baccelliere, Co-ordinators

Tel: 01277 215011

E-mail: info@oases.org.uk

Details: Our vision: 'turning dry ground into springs of water' (Is 41:18b–20) – to refresh, to revive, to make ready!

The Oases are growing communities of young people responding to God's call to radical faith; through this prayer network we are inspiring, equipping and motivating our generation to become the saints of the new millennium! Oasis prayer meetings take place in Birmingham, as well as elsewhere. Each Oasis community meets monthly and contains the four core elements; Fellowship, Adoration, Intercession, and Praise and Worship.

St Chad's Cathedral

Cathedral House, St Chad's, Queensway, Birmingham B4 6EU

Contact: Rev Brian Doolan, Cathedral Dean

Tel: 0121 236 2251   **E-mail:** cathedral.dean@rc-birmingham.org

Details: Sunday Mass 9 am, 11 am, 5 pm. Weekday Mass 12.15 pm and 6 pm. Confessions daily; Sat 10.30–12 noon. Saturday Masses: 10 am, vigil at 4.30 pm. Choir. Shrine of St Chad. RCIA course each year.

North: Chaplaincies

Bradford College, Bradford University

Bradford Catholic University and College Chaplaincy, 1 Ashgrove,
Bradford BD7 1BN
www.student.brad.ac.uk/x11175/

Contact: Rev Dennis Cassidy

Tel: 01274 721636   **E-mail:** catholic-chaplaincy@bradford.ac.uk

Details: The chaplaincy is opposite the Chesham Building.

Catholic Society, Journey in Faith, daily Mass, talks and discussion groups throughout the term, Chaplaincy Club.

Accommodation: 9 rooms available for students.

University of Huddersfield

Chaplaincy Centre, Queensgate Campus, University of Huddersfield HD1 3DH

Contact: Rev Paul Heneghan, Chaplain

Tel: 01484 472 090
E-mail: P.J.Heneghan@hud.ac.uk

Details: Close to main entrance of university – a minute's walk from reception and well signposted. Office, quiet room, drop-in-centre.

Drop-in centre, Mon – Fri, 8 am – 9 pm. Chaplaincy lunch, Mon 12.30 pm. Saturday walks. Cathsoc, Thurs 5:30 pm – 9 pm. Eucharist: Mon – Wed 8:30am; Friday 1pm. Chaplain available Mon – Wed, Fri, 8 am–7 pm and Thurs 5–9 pm. On call through mobile.

Sheffield Hallam University

Catholic Chaplaincy, 18 Broomhall Road, Sheffield S10 2DR

Contact: Rev Alan Williams SM, Chaplain

Tel: 0114 267 9788

Details: The Chaplaincy is two minutes' walk from the collegiate and campus.

Sunday Mass is at 7pm during term time followed by a pound-a-head meal and social for those who can stay. Student support and activities are coordinated by the Chaplain and Chaplaincy Assistants. There is a weekly "Faith Talk" and retreats / pilgrimages are also organised on a regular basis. The Catholic Student Society has one of the largest memberships at the University and organises a lively social calendar (see www.shuxi.org.uk). The Chaplaincy has active links with a nearby Catholic Secondary school Chaplaincy and the youth groups of the local parishes.

Accommodation: There is limited accommodation for students at the Chaplaincy.

University of Sheffield

The Catholic Chaplaincy, 7 Wellesley Road, Sheffield S10 2SY
www.sheffield.ac.uk/ccf

Contact: Rev Peter Cullen, Chaplain

Tel: 0114 266 0178
E-mail: P.J.Cullen@sheffield.ac.uk

Details: Next to Charles Clifford Dental Hospital. Chapel, common room, student kitchen, TV room, full-time Priest Chaplain.

Masses on Sundays: 11.30 am (chaplaincy), 6.30 pm (Earnshaw Hall, University Residence). The Catholic Chaplaincy at the University of Sheffield offers lively worship, great events and an open house for Catholic students and staff and their friends. Full details are available at our website.

Trinity and All Saints College

Chaplaincy, Trinity and All Saints College, Brownberrie Lane, Horsforth,
Leeds L518 5HD

Contact: The Chaplain

Tel: 0113 283 7201

Details: The Chaplaincy lounge is alongside the Chapel, at the the centre of the College.

The chaplaincy is committed to supporting the College's principles of care and community and welcoming students of all races, religions and cultures. The college maintains an active Catholic/Christian life in an atmosphere of freedom and personal responsibility. The College community reflects the multi-faith nature of society and its Catholic Chaplain works to maintain links with Chaplains of all faiths. The campus-based chapel is at the heart of the college, and it is open for prayer, worship or meditation. Alternatively, students have access to a separate prayer room within the College. Students who might wish to seek different arrangements for these purposes should contact the chaplain. (See also the entry for Trinity and All Saints College under 'Catholic Education'.)

Accommodation: Available from the college.

University of York

www.york.ac.uk/univ/chap/

Details: The Catholic Chaplaincy is based at More House on Heslington Lane. Mass is celebrated each weekday in the small upper room chapel. For further details of the provision for Catholic Chaplaincy, please approach the University. For details of the Catholic Students' Society see: www.york.ac.uk/univ/chap/societies/clm_societies.html#cassoc

North: Organisations

Communion and Liberation

www.clonline.org.uk

Contact:

Tel: 0799 0543866
E-mail: cl_uk@onetel.net.uk

Details: Weekly meetings are held in Sheffield where we help each other to share and judge our lives in the light of the encounter with Christ. During the year, national retreats and holidays are organised, with students from universities all around the UK. Please refer to our entry under 'New Movements and Evangelisation' for further information.

Cursillos in Christianity

Clayton House, Newlands Lane, Stoke Row, Henley-on-Thames RG9 5QS
www.cursillo.org.uk

Contact: Mr Stephen Fox, National Secretary

Tel: 01491 681646
E-mail: stephen.fox@cursillo.org.uk

Details: Cursillo is a Catholic movement to form leaders, who grow through prayer, study and action to evangelise others for Christ.

The movement is active in the Diocese of Hallam, and elsewhere. Three-day weekends are run on a Diocesan basis.

Focolare Movement

62 Kings Avenue, London SW4 8BH
www.focolare.org

Contact: Pat Whitney, Communications Assistant

Tel: 0208 671 8355
E-mail: pat@focolare.demon.co.uk

Details: Focolare is an international movement started by Chiara Lubich in Trent, Italy in 1943. Its principal aim is to contribute to the fulfilment of Jesus' prayer. "May they all be one". It is at the service of dialogue within and between churches, with people of different faiths and with those who want to work for peace and unity in all spheres of society. The young people's section, known as Youth for a United World, organises activities in Leeds, as well as elsewhere.

Hallam Catholic Youth Service

Hallam CYS, St Charles Street, Sheffield S9 3WY
www.hallam_diocese.com/youth

Contact: Mr Kevan Grady, Director of Youth Services

Tel: 0114 256 6460 **E-mail:** youthservice@hallam_diocese.com

Details: Hallam Catholic Youth Service is the agency of the diocese of Hallam working with young people aged 18–25. The service offers students opportunities to be involved as volunteer youth workers in a variety of parish settings and opportunities to participate in diocesan pilgrimages to Lourdes and World Youth Day, and other diocesan events.

St Anne's Cathedral

St Anne's Cathedral, Cookridge Street, Leeds

Tel: 0113 245 3626

Details: The cathedral church for the Diocese of Leeds.

St Marie's Cathedral

St Marie's Cathedral, Norfolk Row, Sheffield S1 2JB

Tel: 0114 272 2522

Details: The cathedral church for the Diocese of Hallam.

University of Sheffield Union of Students Pro-life Society

www.shef.ac.uk/pro-life
E-mail: pro-life@shef.ac.uk

Details: If you want to become involved in the most important cause of our day – campaigning for the right to life – as well as meeting lots of friendly young people committed to it, then come and join us at the Pro-life Society. We organise a whole range of campaigning, lobbying, awareness-raising events and activities, including great socials. For further information, please see the website.

North East: Chaplaincies

Durham University

Durham University Catholic Chaplaincy, St Cuthbert's Presbytery, Old Elvet, Durham DH1 3HL
www.stcuthberts.org.uk

Contact: Rev Peter Leighton, Chaplain

Tel: 0191 384 3442

E-mail: peter.leighton@durham.ac.uk

Details: The chaplaincy is part of a wider community of St Cuthbert's Parish which is situated in the centre of Durham City. During term there is a Mass for students every Sunday evening (6.30 pm) at St Cuthbert's Church. Information about other services and events are available on the website. There is also a thriving Catholic Society in Durham which works closely with the Chaplain to offer spiritual, pastoral and social activities for Catholic students. For further information, visit the Catholic Society website, www.durham.ac.uk/cathsoc, or e-mail: Catholic.Society@ durham.ac.uk

Hull University

113–115 Cottingham Road, Hull HU5 2DH

Contact: Rev James O'Brien, Chaplain

Tel: 01482 343216

E-mail: J.H.OBrien@hull.ac.uk

Details: Chapel, prayer room, library, lounge, TV room, kitchen.

Sunday and weekday Masses, Confessions, Exposition, Journey in Faith, Prayer Group, retreats, social activities, talks, full-time chaplain available.

Newcastle University, Northumbria University, Newcastle College of Further Education

RC Chaplaincy, 14 Windsor Terrace, Jesmond, Newcastle upon Tyne NE2 4HE
www.catholicchaplaincy.org

Contact: Rev David Russell and Sr Anne Donockley OSA

Tel: 0191 239 9527 ; 0191 281 1053

E-mail: david.russell@ncl.ac.uk
anne.donockely@unn.ac.uk

Details: Situated off Campus behind the Robinson Library and Newcastle Civic Centre. Chapel, meeting rooms, social space and bar, chaplains' offices, student common room and library.

The Cathsoc Society joins students of all three places together. The Chaplaincy has on Sunday 11am Mass followed by coffee and 6.45pm Mass followed by social in the bar. 8.15am Mon–Fri morning prayer of the 'Northumbria Community' followed by breakfast. Weekday Masses in the chaplaincy 5.15pm Mon–Wed and on Northumbria Campus on Thursday. We arrange one weekend away each term. Every Tuesday Cathsoc have a 'Big Night Out' – including pub, Quasar, ten-pin bowling, cinema, theatre and ice skating at Christmas. Every Thursday students go to help at St Benedict's special needs club in Wallsend. Students hold a Christmas party each year for both the special needs club and for patients at a local psychiatric hospital. Annual Cathsoc dinner. Justice and Peace awareness and events. Wed night 'Emmaus Programme'. Special events for postgraduates. Monthly African Society meeting. Monthly Diocesan Youth Mission Team workshop evening. Weekly RCIA programme. Students are involved in Student LifeNet (see entry under the national listing for 'Other Organisations'). Support for local refugee services. The chaplains are available at all times.

Accommodation: The Chaplaincy houses seven students for a maximum of two years. The students self-cater but we aim to eat together to celebrate birthdays and at Christmas and even more regularly when possible.

Sunderland University

St Mary's Presbytery, 27 Bridge Street, Sunderland SR1 1TQ

Contact: Rev Christopher Jackson, Chaplain

Tel: 0191 567 5354

E-mail: frchrisjackson@gmx.net

Details: St Mary's Church, presbytery and Cathsoc premises (in Parish centre). St Mary's is situated at the south end of the main Wear bridge.

Chaplaincy organises retreats and discussion groups during term. There are sporadic Cathsoc meetings and a monthly student meal. The Chaplain is officially part-time but is always available to students. There has also been student involvement with local projects working with asylum seekers.

Teeside University

Sacred Heart Presbytery, 1 Park Road South, Middlesborough TS5 6LD

Contact: Rev Derek Turnham, Chaplain

Tel: 01642 850113

E-mail: derekturnham@email.msn.com

Details: The Chaplaincy to Teeside University is provided by the Parish of Sacred Heart and St Patrick, working in partnership with chaplains of other denominations. Students are welcomed to Mass at Sacred Heart church and share in other parish activities.

North East: Organisations

Faith Forum, Hull

Ss Mary and Joseph, Baxtergate, Hedon, East Yorkshire HU12 8JN

Contact: Rev William Massie, Chaplain

Tel: 01482 898338 **E-mail:** William.Massie@Wmassie.freeserve.co.uk

Details. Regular programme of talks, retreats and opportunities to meet other young Catholics from Hull and the region.

Newcastle University Pro-life Group

E-mail: DavidEAshby@yahoo.com

Details: We are a small but active group. We campaign within the University and co-operate with other pro-life groups in the locality.

St Mary's Cathedral

St Mary's Cathedral, Clayton Street West, Newcastle-upon-Tyne NE1 5HH

Tel: 0191 232 6953

Details: The cathedral church for the Diocese of Hexham and Newcastle.

St Mary's Cathedral

St Mary's Cathedral, Dalby Way, Coulby Newham, Middlesborough

Tel: 01642 597750

Details: The cathedral church for the Diocese of Middlesborough.

North West: Chaplaincies

Bolton Institute of Higher Education

www.bolton.ac.uk/studentguidance/chaplaincy/index.html

Details: For details of the provision for Catholic chaplaincy, please approach the Institute.

University of Central Lancashire

www.uclan.ac.uk/student_services/faith/churches/preston/catholic.htm

Details: The Multi-Faith Centre is located opposite to the main entrance to the University Library in St Peter's Square. For details of the provision for Catholic chaplaincy, please see the above web page or approach the University.

Lancaster University

The Chaplaincy Centre, Lancaster University, Lancaster LA1 4YW

Contact: Rev Paul Billington and Mr Stephen Hoyland

Tel: 01524 594 079
E-mail: pauleobill@aol.com
s.hoyland@lancaster.ac.uk

Details: Building is central to University and its logo is based on the Chaplaincy towers.

Joint Ecumenical services twice each term, inter-faith forum each term, Freshers' Week activities, three Time Away Retreats per year, week of guided prayer, One World Week, Religious Awareness week, Catholic Society, Alpha, Journey in Faith.

Liverpool Hope University College

The Chaplaincy, Hope University College, Hope Park, Liverpool,

Contact: Sr Claire Sykes FCJ, Chaplain

Tel: 0151 291 3546
E-mail: sykesm2@hope.ac.uk

Details: At the centre of Hope Park Campus just along from the Union.

The ecumenical chaplaincy is a support service at the heart of college life, with the Chaplaincy Base located at the centre of the Hope Park campus. It is dedicated to the wellbeing of all members of the college and the chaplains are committed to supporting the spiritual, social and personal needs and aspirations of all members of the college community. The college itself is an ecumenical institution.

Accommodation: provided by the College.

Liverpool John Moores University, University of Liverpool

Philip Neri House, 30 Catharine St, Liverpool L8 7NL
www.cathchap.org.uk

Contact: Rev Ian McParland, Chaplain

Tel: 0151 709 3858

Details: Serves Liverpool John Moores University and University of Liverpool. For details and information, consult the website.

Manchester Metropolitan University (Alsager Campus)

St Gabriel, 140 Lawton Road, Alsager ST7 2DE

Tel: 01270 872542

Details: Office in the Student Services building, close to the large car park, Alsager Campus.

Availability for one-to-one discussions, queries or assistance in practice of the faith. Masses at weekends take place in St Gabriel's RC Church, Alsager. My limited time at the office is due to my being Parish Priest and Governor of our two schools.

Manchester Metropolitan University, Royal Northern College of Music

St Augustine's Roman Catholic Chaplaincy, All Saints Campus, Grosvenor Square, Manchester M15 6BW
www.saintaugustines.org.uk

Tel: 0161 236 6762
E-mail: augustines@eggconnect.net

Details: Situated in the middle of All Saints Campus – facing Oxford Road and the Students Union. Facilities: beautiful church, shared with small parish; common room; 'Ball' room; kitchen; offices; library; etc.

The source and summit of the chaplaincy timetable is 5pm Sunday Mass, to which all students are welcome. From this flows a variety of activities, from faith discussion to five-a-side, Taizé prayer evenings, and sponsored events for charity. As chaplaincy provision develops, so do links with local parishioners and local charities. Each term a programme of events is published which includes weekends away, concerts involving musicians from the RNCM, whole parish events, RCIA Journey in Faith, opportunities for catechetical instruction, joint events with St Peter's ecumenical chaplaincy, DVD nights, Mass by candlelight and a Summer Ball. Ongoing pastoral support available throughout the term provided by the chaplain, Fr Chris Gorton, Sr Mauraid, Assistant Chaplain, and other members of the team.

University of Manchester

Avila House, 337 Oxford Road, Manchester M13 9GB

orgs.man.ac.uk/Catholic/

Contact: Rev John Broadley

Tel: 0161 273 1456
E-mail: chapsmjb@man.ac.uk

Details: Opposite University of Manchester Students Union on Oxford Road. Chapel, lounge and library.

Chaplaincy is joint with UMIST. Weekday Mass and lunch. Coffee after Sunday mass at Holy Name Church. Residential retreats. Commitment to Third World. Social activities. Prayer group with teaching input. Chaplain freely available. Pro-life society at students union. Rite for the Christian Initiation of Adults. Encouragement given for student initiatives. Maintains a presence in university.

University of Salford

www.salford.ac.uk/religion/

Details: The main ecumenical chaplaincy centre is in the Chapman building, Peel campus. For details of the provision for Catholic chaplaincy, please approach the University.

U.M.I.S.T.

orgs.man.ac.uk/Catholic/

Details: For details of the Catholic chaplaincy provision, please approach the University. See also entry for the University of Manchester.

North West: Organisations

Catholic Caring Services

218 Tulketh Road, Preston PR2 1ES
www.catholiccaringservices.org.uk

Contact: Mr Mark Wiggin, Principal Officer, Community Services

Tel: 01772 732313 **E-mail:**
info@catholiccaringservices.org.uk

Details: Catholic Caring Services offers, in Lancashire and Cumbria, volunteering opportunities to students, work experience placements for social work / care professions and an information service that can point students towards paid and voluntary work within organisations and services that have a Christian ethos. Subject matter for appropriate research projects from students can occasionally be provided.

Catholic Children's Rescue Society

390 Parrs Wood Road, Didsbury, Manchester M20 5NA

Contact: Volunteer Co-Ordinator

Tel: 0161 445 7741
E-mail: ccrs@lineone.net

Details: This Salford Diocesan charity provides support services to children and families, supported accommodation for homeless young women and their children, a family placement service, respite care for children with disabilities, and children's homes for those in the care of the local authorities. In addition, two charity shops work for us in a fundraising capacity. Opportunities for volunteers exist across the organisation.

Catholic Welfare Societies (Inc), Diocese of Salford

390 Parrs Wood Road, Manchester, M20 5NA

Contact: Tony Murray, Executive Office

Tel: 0161 445 7741
E-mail: ccrs@lineone.net

Details: Volunteering opportunities (in conjunction with other organisations) that are available for students in Greater Manchester include: services for the homeless, deaf people, disabled people and the elderly; residential care homes; children's hospice; and work placements for professional Social Work students.

Communion and Liberation

www.clonline.org.uk

Tel: 0799 0543866
E-mail: cl_uk@onetel.net.uk

Details: Weekly meetings are held in Liverpool and Manchester where we help each other to share and judge our lives in the light of the encounter with Christ. During the year national retreats and holidays are organised, with students from universities all around the UK. Please refer to our entry under 'New Movements and Evangelisation' for further information.

Coniston Hall

67–77 Hathersage Road, Manchester M13 0EW
www.conistonhall.org.uk

Contact: Eileen Cole, Director

Tel: 0161 248 5585
E-mail: info@conistonhall.org.uk

Details: Hall of residence for women students of any denomination. Mass is celebrated daily. The chaplain is often available for consultation/spiritual guidance. Talks and seminars on relevant topics. Pastoral care entrusted to the Opus Dei Prelature. Organisers of the Reach Out! Inner-city Youth Achievement Programme for girls.

Cornerstone Day Care Centre

104B Denmark Road, Manchester M15 6JS

Contact: Br John Sullivan

Tel: 0161 232 8888

Details: The centre is run by the Catholic Welfare Societies and is usually open between 10am and 4pm. It offers facilities such as a café, shower and shaving, laundry and clothing shop. Volunteers are welcome to assist the staff of this day-care centre in meeting the needs of homeless, disadvantaged and isolated adults.

Covenant Prayer Community

30 Tarnside Close, Smallbridge, Rochdale, Lancashire OL16 2QD

Contact: Mr Christopher Power, Community Leader

Tel: 01706 640359
E-mail: candm@power.freeisp.co.uk

Details: A non-residential Catholic community with an ecumenical dimension. Members live and work in different places and belong to different churches and denominations. The community lives its faith through prayer, commitment, support and social justice. Its activities include charismatic prayer meetings, 'flame nights' (spiritual refreshment with prayer, worship, teaching and healing), contemplative prayer through scripture, and men's evenings. It offers practical support through helping to organise and lead 'Alpha', 'CaFE' and 'Life in the Spirit' courses, workshops, liturgies, informal prayer times and advice sessions.

Cursillos in Christianity

Clayton House, Newlands Lane, Stoke Row, Henley-on-Thames RG9 5QS
www.cursillo.org.uk

Contact: Mr Stephen Fox, National Secretary

Tel: 01491 681646
E-mail: stephen.fox@cursillo.org.uk

Details: Cursillo is a Catholic movement to form leaders, who grow through prayer, study and action to evangelise others for Christ. The movement is active in the Diocese of Liverpool, and elsewhere. Three-day weekends are run on a diocesan basis.

Diocese of Lancaster Services to Young People

St. Joseph's Presbytery, Syne Road, Skerton, Lancaster LA1 2HU

Contact: Miss Anne Kennedy, Advisor for work with young people

Tel: 01524 848182
E-mail: LancasterDYS@aol.com

Details: Opportunities to offer their services to support youth work locally. Places to meet, should they wish to create a network. Access to training and resources for youth work or their involvement in organising prayer and liturgy for themselves. One- and two-year work opportunities post-university in a residential setting and also working in local parish communities. (See entry under 'Gap Years' for Castlerigg Manor.)

Focolare Movement

14 Sinclair Drive, Liverpool L18 0HN

Contact: Mr Mike Beresford, Youth Assistant

Tel: 0151 722 3981
E-mail: m_beresford@yahoo.com

Details: Focolare is an international movement started by Chiara Lubich in Trent, Italy in 1943. Its principal aim is to contribute to the fulfilment of Jesus' prayer, "May they all be one". It is at the service of dialogue within and between churches, with people of different faiths and with those who want to work for peace and unity in all spheres of society. The young people's section, known as Youth for a United World, organises activities in Liverpool and elsewhere.

Greygarth Hall

1 Lower Park Road, Manchester M13 9PL
www.greygarth.org.uk

Contact: Xavier Bosch, Warden

Tel: 0161 224 2582
E-mail: secretary@greygarth.org.uk

Details: Located very near the universities, the Hall offers male students clean, comfortable bedrooms and superb study facilities including a computer suite, a library and a seminar room. Greygarth organises a number of cultural and sporting events. Daily mass, talks and conferences on the Catholic Faith are given by the resident chaplain. Open to people of all faiths and none. Spiritual activities are entrusted to Opus Dei, a prelature of the Church.

Holy Name Church

Oxford Road, Manchester M13 9PG

Contact: Rev Ray Matus

Tel: 0161 273 2435

Details: Mass, Confessions, Exposition and Benediction of the Blessed Sacrament all occur at least once each day from Monday to Saturday. There are three Sunday Masses, which also serve students at the University of Manchester and UMIST. Choir: The St Philip Neri Singers sing about five times each term for the major feast days.

Metropolitan Cathedral of Christ the King

Cathedral House, Mount Pleasant, Liverpool L3 5TQ
www.liverpoolmetrocathedral.org.uk

Contact: Mgr Peter Cookson, Cathedral Dean

Tel: 0151 709 9222
E-mail: met.cathedral@aucom.net

Details: The Cathedral is situated at the heart of the campuses of the universities and serves as parish church to very many students. It offers a wide variety of liturgical styles and Mass times, the Saturday vigil and Sunday evening Masses being particularly popular with students.

Neocatechumenal Way, North West

Contact: Paul Allen
Tel: 0151 495 3259

Details: The Neocatechumenal Way is an itinerary of Catholic formation which, lived in small communities within the parish, helps people to rediscover and to live the immense riches of their baptism. After an initial set of teachings on the Catholic faith, those who wish to do so will form and continue as a community which then meets on a regular basis to celebrate together the Liturgy of the Word and the Eucharist, going through various stages similar to those of the 'catechumenate' of the Early Church. The Neocatechumenal Way is governed by a Statute approved by the Holy See.

ReachOut!

30 Selworthy Road, Moss Side, Manchester M16 7AH
www.reachoutuk.org

Contact: Mr Mike Tomsky, Student Volunteers Manager

Tel: 0161 2267633
E-mail: mtomsky@reachoutuk.org

Details: ReachOut! exists to enthuse young people (aged between 9 and 16) in deprived areas about education and personal development. Student volunteers act as mentors to young people on a one-to-one basis. The volunteers help the young people in their school work, but their role goes beyond that of transferring knowledge: they are role models, and as well as academic development they work on other areas such as social and emotional development. Full training is offered to the volunteers on a variety of areas (from first aid to teaching methods) to enable them to make a real impact on the lives of the young people involved.

Work done for ReachOut! is recognised by Millennium Volunteers and the Duke of Edinburgh Award schemes. Female students interested in volunteering should contact Coniston Hall (see entry for Coniston Hall below).

Salford Cathedral Centre

250 Chapel St, Salford M3 5LL

Contact: Sr Angela O' Connor, Project Co-Ordinator

Tel: 0161 839 4191
E-mail: aoconnor@shcj.org

Details: Salford Cathedral Centre is a drop-in centre for homeless and disadvantaged people. It offers students an opportunity to be actively involved in the life of the Church by serving those in need in our society. This service can be done in different ways, by volunteering on a regular basis a few hours a week, or by giving a gap year through the Jesuit Volunteer Community or the Vincentian Volunteer community. Students can also do pastoral and community placements.

St Benedict's Monastery

St. Benedict's Monastery, Convent Close, Bamber Bridge PR5 6US

Contact: Rev Dom Colin Battell, Prior

Tel: 01772 902208

E-mail: cbattell@ukonline.co.uk

Details: The monastery is a dependent Priory of the Benedictine monastery of St. Lawrence at Ampleforth. St Benedict's has contact with students through its chaplaincy work at Cardinal Newman College, Preston. Students are welcome to visit the monastery or stay at the Guest House at nominal charge. For further details, please contact the Prior.

St John's RC Cathedral

250 Chapel Street, Salford M3 5LL

Contact: Rev John Dale, Cathedral Dean

Tel: 0161 834 0333
E-mail: cathedral@salforddiocese.org

Details: Vibrant Sunday Liturgy – 11am Mass. Quiet reflective Sunday Liturgy – 5.30pm Mass. Multi-cultural atmosphere, warm welcome, good bookshop with variety of resources. Our Cathedral drop-in centre is always looking for volunteers to help in the care of the homeless (see entry for Salford Cathedral Centre).

St Peter's Cathedral

St Peter's Cathedral, East Road Lancaster LA1 3BT

Tel: 01524 61860

Details: The cathedral church for the Diocese of Lancaster.

St Wilfrid's Parish Church

1 Winckley Square, Preston PR1 3JJ
www.saintwilfred.org.uk

Contact: David Birchall SJ, Parish Priest

Tel: 01772 555886
E-mail: info@saintwilfrid.org.uk

Details: Busy city-centre church open all day every day. Convenient Mass and confession times. Occasional student events. Periodic courses in theology and faith. Music group welcomes new members. Jesuit-run parish.

Scotland: Chaplaincies

Aberdeen University

Details: For details of the provision for Catholic Chaplaincy, please approach the University.

Dundee University

www.catholic-forum.com/churches/stac/catsoc/index.html

Details: Dundee University has a purpose-built ecumenical chaplaincy centre that is located at the centre of the main University campus. As well as a chapel there is a coffee bar, common room, library, quiet room and the Chaplains' offices. See also: www.dundee.ac.uk/chaplaincy/ . For details of the provision for Catholic chaplaincy, please approach the University.

Dundee, University of Abertay

Details: Please approach the University for details of the provision for Catholic chaplaincy.

Edinburgh University and Edinburgh College of Art

23–24 George Square, Edinburgh EH8 9LD
www.scotland.op.org/edinburgh/chaplaincy

Contact: Rev Simon Francis Gaine OP and Rev Peter Hunter OP

Tel: 0131 650 0904 **E-mail:** edinburgh.chaplain@scotland.op.org

Details: The Chaplaincy is located in George Square near the university library

and several other university buildings. There is a chapel, dining area, comfy common room, a kitchen and a large garden. The common room is open 24 hours a day to members of the Catholic Students' Union.

There is a student Mass with music provided by students at 7.15pm on Sundays in term. The Catholic Students' Union organises weekly talks and discussions on the Catholic faith, a weekly 'Fellowship Meal' cooked by students, prayer group and Bible study, various social events and a termly retreat. There is also the daily opportunity to join in the prayer of the Dominican community which has served the Chaplaincy since 1931.

Glasgow Caledonian University

www.saintmungo.org

Details: For details of the provision for Catholic chaplaincy, please see the above web page or approach the University.

Glasgow University

Turnbull Hall, 15 Southpark Terrace, Glasgow G12 8LG
www.gla.ac.uk/clubs/Turnbull/turnbull.html

Contact: Rev John Keenan, Chaplain

Tel: 0141 339 4315

E-mail: RCChaplaincy@gla.ac.uk

Details: Turnbull Hall is a large Catholic Chaplaincy on the university campus, owned and funded by the Archdiocese of Glasgow. Off University Avenue at the reading room 100 yards along.

Sunday Masses: Sat 6.15pm, Sun 11.30am and 6.45pm, Daily Masses: Mon–Fri 1.05pm. Confession: Wed and Fri 12.45pm. Rosary: Mon–Fri 8am and 12.45pm. Prayer Group: Wed 6pm. Facilities: Free lunch (soup/pasta, tea and coffee). Internet Café: free access to university students. Free tea & coffee, plus fridge and microwave. Lounge: Satellite TV, EWTN,

Sky, Video & DVD, Newspapers. Study room: for 18 students; newly refurbished.

Accommodation: Student flats for six students (three flats, two sharing). Newly refurbished. Leases for registered Glasgow students are from October–June at £52 per week. Leases during summer can be arranged.

Heriot Watt University

www.hw.ac.uk/chaplaincy/

Details: The ecumenical Chaplaincy is located at the top of the Walk, near to the Mathematics and Civil/Offshore Departments. Please approach the University for details of the provision for Catholic chaplaincy.

Napier University

www.napier.ac.uk/support/personal.asp?pageid=3

Details: Please approach the University for details of the provision for Catholic chaplaincy.

Robert Gordon University

www.rgu.ac.uk/studentservices/chaplaincy/

Details: The University provides a Chaplaincy service on an ecumenical basis with links to all the major churches and faith groups in Aberdeen. For details of the provision for Catholic chaplaincy, please approach the University.

University of St Andrews

St James, 17 The Scores, St Andrews, Scotland KY16 9AR

Contact: Very Rev Brian M. Canon Halloran BD MPhil PhD, Chaplain

Tel: 01334 472856

E-mail: bmh4@st-and.ac.uk

Details: Canmore, 24 The Scores, St Andrews. Opposite Catholic Church.

Mass in chaplaincy: Wednesday evening (7.30pm); Friday evening (5.30pm). Catholic Students Society meets Wednesday evening (8pm). Rite for the Christian Initiation of Adults (RCIA) meets Monday evening (8pm).

University of Stirling

www.chaplaincy.stir.ac.uk/

Details: For details of the provision for Catholic chaplaincy, please approach the University.

University of Strathclyde

Chaplaincy Centre, St Paul's Building, 90 John Street, Glasgow G1 1JH

Contact: Rev Brendan Slevin OP BA MA, Chaplain

Tel: 0141 548 2728
E-mail: brendan@strath.ac.uk

Details: Location: opposite Strathclyde students' union. Chapel, common room, two meeting rooms, small library and a café open throughout the day. Ecumenical Chaplaincy Centre.

Weekday lunchtime Mass. Sunday Mass 11am, followed by coffee. Occasional Sunday meals after mass. Catholic Society, organized retreats, Scripture study group, Taizé prayer group, Ecumenical faith questions group. Being an ecumenical chaplaincy gives an opportunity to meet, discuss and worship with Christians of other denominations. Other Catholic groups that use chaplaincy include the Newman Association (Glasgow circle) and the Glasgow Lay Dominicans.

Scotland: Organisations

Aberdeen Diocesan Youth Service

Diocesan Youth Office, 3A Hill Park, Inverness IV2 4AL
www.rcdays.co.uk

Contact: Mrs Marie Cooke, Diocesan youth Co-Ordinator

Tel: 01463 232136
E-mail: youthoffice@supanet.com

Details: This is the Youth Service of Aberdeen Diocese which stretches from Shetland to Aviemore and from coast to coast. We provide info and support, social and spiritual events for young people (aged 5–30) including students at our universities and colleges.

Ambassadors for Christ (Community of the Risen Christ)

Community of the Risen Christ, P.O. Box 26304, Clarkston, Glasgow G76 8YU
www.risenchrist.org.uk

Contact: Mr John Hempsey, Coordinator

Tel: 0141 423 3445
E-mail: afc@risenchrist.org.uk

Details: Ambassadors for Christ is part of the Community of the Risen Christ, a lay covenant community based in Glasgow (part of an international community of communities, known as the Sword of the Spirit). Locally we have a vibrant group of young students who meet weekly to share and pray and have fellowship together – offering each other support in the Christian life. AfC is frequently involved in outreach work to local schools and to students at university and college.

Cathedral of St Mary of the Assumption

Cathedral of St Mary of the Assumption, Huntly Street, Aberdeen

Tel: 01224 640160

Details: The cathedral church for the Diocese of Aberdeen.

Communion and Liberation

www.clonline.org.uk

Tel: 0799 0543866
E-mail: cl_uk@onetel.net.uk

Details: Weekly meetings are held in Glasgow where we help each other to share and judge our lives in the light of the encounter with Christ. During the year national retreats and holidays are organised, with students from universities all around the UK. Please refer to our entry under 'New Movements and Evangelisation' for further information.

Dunreath Study Centre

231 Nithsdale Road, Glasgow G41 5HA

Contact: Mr Dermot Grenham, Director

Tel: 0141 427 3236
E-mail: dermotg@dunreath.clara.net

Details: Dunreath study centre provides students with an environment in which they can study without distractions in a well stocked library. We organise seminars and talks on topics of interest to students. We also run Citywise, a service project with immigrant children. The spiritual activities (such as meditations, recollections and retreats) are entrusted to Opus Dei.

Focolare Movement

30 Langside Drive, Glasgow G43 2QQ
www.focolare.org

Contact: Irene Jovaras

Tel: 0141 637 3316
E-mail: focolareglasgow@Freenet.co.uk

Details: Focolare is an international movement started by Chiara Lubich in Trent, Italy in 1943. Its principal aim is to contribute to the fulfilment of Jesus' prayer, "May they all be one". It is at the service of dialogue within and between churches, with people of different faiths and with those who want to work for peace and unity in all spheres of society. The young people's section, known as Youth for a United World, organises activities in Glasgow and Edinburgh, as well as elsewhere.

Glenalvon

5 Kirklee Gardens, Glasgow G12 0SG

Contact: Anne Williams, Secretary

Tel: 0141 339 3234
E-mail: Glenalvon@ntlworld.com

Details: Glenalvon is close to Glasgow University and offers good accommodation and study facilities for female students. It hosts cultural talks as well as conferences on the Catholic faith. It organises volunteers to help in after-school clubs in deprived areas of Glasgow. There are also opportunities to take part in voluntary projects overseas in summer, such as teaching English in Estonia or participating in rural projects in Africa. Work placements can also be organised for the Gap Year. Other activities include hill walking, study weekends and retreats. The pastoral care and activities in Glenalvon are entrusted to the Opus Dei Prelature.

Neocatechumenal Way, Glasgow

Contact: Jim and Kath McGoldrig

Tel: 0141 774 7620
E-mail: dingab1@hotmail.com

Details: The Neocatechumenal Way is an itinerary of Catholic formation which, lived in small communities within the parish, helps people to rediscover and to live the immense riches of their baptism. After an initial set of teachings on the Catholic faith, those who wish to do so will form and continue as a community which then meets on a regular basis to celebrate together the Liturgy of the Word and the Eucharist, going through various stages similar to those of the 'catechumenate' of the Early Church. The Neocatechumenal Way is governed by a Statute approved by the Holy See.

Pluscarden Abbey

Pluscarden Abbey, Pluscarden, Elgin, Moray IV30 8UA
www.pluscardenabbey.org

Contact: Rev Giles Conacher OSB, Prior

Tel: 01343 890257
E-mail: monks@pluscardenabbey.org

Details: Pluscarden Abbey is a community of Benedictine monks. It offers its retreat houses for men, women and groups, for individual or group use, for prayer and retreat, study, a break, time to think, a chance to seek advice. There is no charge for staying at the Abbey, although donations are not refused! All its services are open to everyone, to share our prayer. It offers community, rural peace and a library.

St Andrews Cathedral

St Andrews Cathedral, Clyde Street, Glasgow

Tel: 0141 221 3096

Details: The cathedral church for the Archdiocese of Glasgow.

St Andrew's Cathedral

St Andrew's Cathedral, Nethergate, Dundee

Tel: 01382 225228

Details: The cathedral church for the Diocese of Dunkeld.

St Mary's Cathedral

61 York Pl., Edinburgh EH1 3JD

Contact: Mgr David Gemmell, Administrator

Tel: 0131 556 0027

Details: Young adults group. Social events. International evenings. Weekend retreats. 7.30pm Sunday Mass with gathering after. St Mary's RC Cathedral is in the heart of Edinburgh city centre. All the Sunday celebrations of Holy Mass attract very cosmopolitan congregations. Hundreds of students make it their spiritual home and are encouraged to join in the social and spiritual life of the parish. The 7.30pm Sunday evening draws together young adults from all across the city. A variety of social and spiritual activities are organised through the year.

St Michael Centre

St Michael's, Main Street, Totmintoul, Moray AB37 9EX
www.saintmikes.co.uk

Contact: Rev Colin Stewart, Warden and Parish Priest

Tel: 01807 580 226
E-mail: warden@saintmikes.co.uk

Details: 34-bed hostel, hired to one group at a time (therefore, groups only). Space for reflection and/or retreats (groups bring own leaders). On site – art, craft, music, astronomy, extensive studios and workshop facilities – well resourced.

St Mirin's Cathedral

St Mirin's Cathedral, Incle Street, Paisley

Tel: 0141 889 2404

Details: The cathedral church for the Diocese of Paisley.

South East: Chaplaincies

Anglia Polytechnic University (Cambridge Campus)

The Catholic Rectory, Hills Road, Cambridge CB2 1JR
www.olem.org.uk

Contact: Rev Rafael Esteban, Chaplain, and Antoinette Askin, Assistant Chaplain

Tel: 01223 350787
E-mail: office@olem.org.uk

Details: Campus chaplaincy office is located in Room 95 of the Ruskin Building, access via Student Lounge. The Rectory is sited next to the church in Hills Road, about a 10-minute walk from campus.

Monthly social gathering on first Sunday of each month after 5pm (term time only). Pastoral care is provided by chaplain and his assistant from the Rectory, Hills Road. Spiritual support and guidance are available from other members of the parish team in the absence of the chaplain / his assistant. Monthly internet newsletter. Chaplain is available on campus on Fridays from 1–3pm. At all other times, he is at the Rectory. Assistant chaplain is available on campus each Monday from 10am–2.30pm and each Wednesday from 2–5.30pm. 'Five Alive' group – musicians and singers who organise the musical input for Sunday Youth Mass. OLEM Choir – provides music for 10.45am Sunday Mass. Both groups meet socially in addition to their practice sessions.

Anglia Polytechnic University (Chelmsford Campus)

90 The Chaplaincy Centre, 31 Park Road, Chelmsford, Essex CM1 1LL
www.apu.ac.uk/thechaplaincy/

Contact: Rev Frank Jackson (Catholic Chaplain) and Rev Ivor Moody (Full-time Chaplain)

Tel: 01245 493131
E-mail: f.j.jackson@apu.ac.uk ; i.r.moody@apu.ac.uk

Details: Semi-detached house on campus, which acts as a drop-in centre. Facilities: tea, coffee, light snack, music room, quiet room and library.

The ecumenical chaplaincy is here for all, irrespective of religious conviction. The Chaplaincy Centre is a great meeting place. Each day starts with morning prayer at 8.30am available in the Chaplaincy Centre and Rivermead. There are services, including Mass, throughout the semesters. There is increased shared activities with the local churches. The Chaplaincy also arranges events which are purely social and fun. Volunteering opportunities are also available.

Accommodation: Hospitality arranged with local families, especially for international students.

Bournemouth University and the Arts Institute at Bournemouth

www.bournemouth.ac.uk/chaplaincy/

Details: For details of the provision for Catholic Chaplaincy to both institutions, please approach the Religion & Faith Service at the University.

Brighton University and Sussex University

Howard House, 2 Station Approach, Falmer, Brighton BN1 9SD

Contact: Rev Rob Esdaile and Sr Blandaid McCauley SSL

Tel: 01273 698032
E-mail: catholicsussex@aol.com

Details: Howard House is opposite Falmer Railway Station entrance and contains a meeting room/library, a residence for seven students and a chaplain's flat.

A fully-functioning university chaplaincy, with its own residential base and meeting room, and use of ecumenical facilities in both universities' campuses. Sunday Mass is at 6pm at the Meeting House of the University of Sussex. Mass (at various different times) is celebrated during the week. Taizé Prayer, faith-sharing and catechectical groups, meals, socials, an annual retreat, pilgrimages and 'SVP Soc' social action are all part of the life of this very international community. All are welcome.

Accommodation: Seven rooms in a self-catering unit.

University of Buckingham

Details: For details of the Catholic chaplaincy provision, please approach the University.

Cambridge University

Cambridge University Catholic Chaplaincy, Fisher House, Cambridge CB2 3NH
www.fisherhouse.org.uk

Contact: Rev Alban McCoy OFM Conv, Rev Stephen Ortiger OSB, Sr Pauline Burling OP, Chaplains

Tel: 01223 742192
E-mail: am335@cam.ac.uk

Details: Chapel, library, daily lunch, tea and coffee available all day. Centrally located next to Corn Exchange, Guildhall,

Machet Hill. House open by means of combination all day and evening.

Large range of groups, all under the aegis of the Fisher Society – student-run, annually elected committee. Termly courses led by chaplains and senior members. Out-reach groups, e.g. CAMALT, small third world projects, CAFOD, Children's Visiting Group, medical ethics discussion group, R.H. Benson Society (graduates society), Signs of the Times discussion group for senior members and graduates, Schola Cantorum, Latin Choir, Bible Study Group.

Cranfield University

St. Mary's Church, Aspley Hill,
Woburn Sands MK17 8NN
pages.zoom.co.uk/stmarys/

Contact: Rev Canon S Codon, Chaplain

Tel: 01908 583 195
E-mail: scond@btinternet.com

Details: The chaplaincy is located within the University Chapel.

Chaplain to Cranfield University. Offers Mass, Eucharistic Services and meetings.

University of East Anglia

Roman Catholic Chaplaincy, University of East Anglia, Norwich NR4 7TJ
www.uea.ac.uk/chaplaincy/catholic.htm

Contact: Mrs Marion Houssart, Lay Chaplain

Tel: 01603 592168
E-mail: m.houssart@uea.ac.uk

Details: Overlooking the square in the middle of campus. Two floors: worship room and quiet rooms upstairs. Office, Common Room, Kitchen and Library downstairs. Open in term time from 8am until late.

On the Catholic side: the Catholic community on campus is a mixture of students and staff engaged in a wide range of disciplines and originating from across

the world. They worship and often socialise together and with others on campus. Mass: Sunday 6pm and Thursday 1.05pm, both in term time (see website for details). For times of confession, RCIA (teaching of the faith), morning prayer, and Rosary – see website. Termly day of recollection, or retreat. Socials such as meals out, days away, parties, as well as social action. In general: although faith is our driving force, it is not a prerequisite for making use of the chaplaincy. It is a place where you are not judged, but accepted for who you are. The chaplaincy falls under the Dean of Students Office as part of student support services. As such there are good links with the whole support network within the university. Common Room with kitchen – a meeting place at the heart of campus – open all day every day in term. Quiet Room to find that place of stillness that we all need from time to time. Ecumenical retreat once per year; university carol service and relevant other events. Three full-time chaplains – Anglican, Catholic and Methodist – are around most of the time and offer a listening ear and a cup of coffee. Visit the website for more information. Visit us on your open day – you will be very welcome!

University of Essex

www2.essex.ac.uk/chaplaincy/

Details: Catholic services are held in the Multi-Faith Chaplaincy Centre, which is located on floor 3, from entrance 9 off square 2. For further details of the Catholic chaplaincy provision, please approach the University.

University of Hertfordshire

www.herts.ac.uk/extrel/UGP2001/frontend/help_advice.html

Details: For details of the provision for Catholic chaplaincy, please approach the University.

University of Kent

St John Stone House, 41 St Thomas Hill, Canterbury, Kent CT2 7NS
www.cathsoc.co.uk

Contact: Rev Peter Geldard, Chaplain

Tel: 01227 823348
E-mail: P.J.Geldard@ukc.ac.uk

Details: St John Stone House (Chaplaincy) is on the edge of campus, at the end of University Road. Common room, bar, The Barque Inn, large kitchen and chapel. The Chaplain's Office is in Elliot College.

Our Sunday Mass (attendance 200+) takes place at 11.30am at the Franciscan International Study Centre, Giles Lane (opposite the University Medical Centre), followed by our 'Pot-Luck Lunch' (attendance 60+) at St John Stone House. Tuesday night Cathsoc meeting (attendance 70). Social activities (attendance 150+).

Accommodation: Accommodation for three students and the chaplain at St John Stone House.

University of Luton

www.luton.ac.uk/studentresources/chaplaincy.shtml

Details: The ecumenical Chaplaincy Centre is situated in Vicarage Street, near to the Student Centre. For details of the Catholic chaplaincy provision, please approach the University.

Northampton, University College

22 Park Avenue North,
Northampton NN3 2HS
www.northampton.ac.uk/stu/general/
chap.html

Contact: Rev Andrew J Behrens, Chaplain

Tel: 01604 713015

Details: The Chaplaincy is sited in the building known as 'Oundle', which is the Student Services building, near the bookshop and the medical centre.

The Chaplaincy acts as an ecumenical team providing support, spiritual and pastoral care to students. The entire team is voluntary and part-time, and Catholic students are invited to attend Mass at one of the many local Catholic churches in Northampton. The Chaplaincy is staffed over lunchtime each week-day.

Oxford Brookes University

62 London Road, Headington,
Oxford OX3 7PD

Contact: Rev Martin Flatman and Sr Veronica Ann

Tel: 01865 750463
E-mail: meflatman@brookes.ac.uk

Details: House with small chapel 10 minutes' walk towards Headington shops. Meeting rooms and student accommodation.

Sunday Mass 6pm with food and drink after; Saturday Mass (for Sunday), 5pm during term; Weekday Mass on campus; annual retreat; prayer group; full-time chaplain always available; help in finding local Catholic church; chaplain works ecumenically on campus with other chaplains from chaplaincy room there.

Accommodation: Four study bedrooms with shared kitchens and bathroom.

Oxford University

Oxford University Catholic Chaplaincy,
The Old Palace, Rose Place, St Aldate's,
Oxford OX1 1RD
www.oucathchap.org.uk

Contact: Rev Jeremy Fairhead,
Rev Neil Ferguson OP, Sr Nora Coughlan
SMG, Rev Paul King

Tel: 01865 276993
E-mail: cathchap@herald.ox.ac.uk

Details: Liturgical: There are three Sunday Masses, two Masses each weekday and one Saturday Mass. Well-known preachers often preside at the 11.00am Sunday Mass. Morning Prayer occurs from Mon–Fri. Regular opportunities for the Sacrament of Reconciliation. The chaplaincy has two choirs. Adoration of the Eucharist occurs each weekday, with Night Prayer and Benediction each Monday evening. The Rosary is recited each Wednesday and Friday. Preparation group for Baptism, Confirmation and Reception into the Church. Weekly meetings: Questioning Catholics; Prayer Group; Newman Society; Pro-life Society; University Catholic Society. Pastoral: lunch each weekday after Mass; Chaplains 'at home' each afternoon and on Monday evening; a place to meet for Catholic graduate students; Society of St Vincent de Paul. Special Events: each term a range of special events is offered, such as retreats, seminars, socials, Salsa nights, and so on.

Accommodation: Please consult the chaplain.

Plater College

Plater College, Pullens Lane,
Oxford OX3 0DT
www.plater.ac.uk

Contact: Mgr J R N Mullin, Chaplain

Tel: 01865 740500
E-mail: jrnm@plater.ac.uk

Details: Chapel, resident Chaplain available to students daily.

Plater College Chapel open every day. Weekday Mass. Training in liturgical ministries. Commitment to Catholic Social Teaching and social justice. Prayer groups, Encouragement of student initiatives. (See also entry for Plater College under 'Catholic Education'.)

Accommodation: 78 study bedrooms in residential college with full board.

Reading University

www.rdg.ac.uk/chaplaincy/cc/
activities.htm

Details: For details of the provision for Catholic chaplaincy, please approach the University.

Southampton Institute

Verbum Dei, Old Saints Hall, 425
Wincester Road, Southampton SO16 7DE

Contact: Sr Maeve Heaney, Chaplain

Tel: 023 8039 9301
E-mail: Maeve.Heaney@solent.ac.uk
maeve@verbum-dei.co.uk

Details: Part of Institute main building: office and quiet room. Area of student service.

Chaplain's presence at institute is part-time (Wed morning and Fri afternoon), but flexible at other times. Links with local parish and other Catholic students. Faith discussion meetings – weekly, Sunday night after Mass. Monthly student mass. Socials with other students/young people. Retreats/encounters organised with and by students.

Accommodation: House beside local parish open to students wishing to be close to local church and to get to know other Christian/Catholic students.

Southampton University

346 Portswood Road,
Southampton SO17 3SB

Contact: Rev Michael Ryan OMI, Chaplain

Tel: 023 8055 9481

E-mail: mjryan_98@yahoo.com

Details: Chaplaincy building is on the main campus opposite the Nuffield Theatre.

The chaplaincy is based at Southampton University (52 University Rd, Highfield, Southampton, SO17 1BJ) and is shared with the Anglican and Free Church chaplains. Cathsoc is well organised (70 members). Mass followed by meal on Sundays at 6.30pm in the chaplaincy. Weekday Masses on Tuesday and Friday at 1pm. Taizé Prayer and Faith Development held on Tuesdays. Cathsoc social events and talks arranged during the term (eg. ten-pin bowling and film nights).

Suffolk College, Ipswich

64 Corder Road, Ipswich, Suffolk IP4 2XB

Contact: Mrs Sue Bell MA MA, Chaplain

Tel: 01473 253858

Details: Two inter-connecting rooms. Meetings; for prayer, discussions, videos, can take place for up to 12 people. No chapel – Catholic Church nearby, with Thursday midday Mass and light lunch, and which also has a library.

The Chaplaincy is inter-denominational, but I represent the Catholic Church, supported by the local parish priest. I am a voluntary part-timer, there regularly on Fridays before 2pm – otherwise available on request, as we live quite nearby and in college for various chaplaincy meetings and college functions.

University of Surrey

www.surrey.ac.uk/Chaplains/CathSoc/index.htm

Details: The ecumenical Chaplaincy is based in Senate House. For details of the provision for Catholic chaplaincy, please see the above web page or approach the University.

Thames Valley University (Slough Campus)

St. Ethelbert's Roman Catholic Church, Wellington Street, Slough SL1 1XU

Contact: Miss Maria Corcoran, Parish Worker

Tel: 01753 523147

E-mail: saintethelberts@ukgateway.net

South East: Organisations

Blackfriars

Buckingham Road, Cambridge CB3 0DD
www.che2.com/blackfriarscambridge/

Contact: Rev Aidan Nichols OP, Prior

Tel: 01223 741251

Details: Divine Office (sung), in novitiate house of English Dominican Province; good preaching; talks on theology (usually in Lent Term).

Cathedral of Our Lady and St Thomas

Cathedral of Our Lady and St Thomas, Kingsthorpe Road, Northampton

Details: The cathedral church for the Diocese of Northampton.

Cathedral of St John the Baptist

Cathedral of St John the Baptist, St Giles' Gate, Norwich

Tel: 01603 624615

Details: The cathedral church for the Diocese of East Anglia.

Cathedral of St Mary and St Helen

Cathedral of St Mary and St Helen, Ingrave Road, Brentwood, Essex,

Tel: 01277 210107

Details: The cathedral church for the Diocese of Brentwood.

Communion and Liberation

www.clonline.org.uk

Tel: 0799 0543866
E-mail: cl_uk@onetel.net.uk

Details: Weekly meetings are held in Oxford, Cambridge and Portsmouth where we help each other to share and judge our lives in the light of the encounter with Christ. During the year national retreats and holidays are organised, with students from universities all around the UK. Please refer to our entry under 'New Movements and Evangelisation' for further information.

Cursillos in Christianity

Clayton House, Newlands Lane, Stoke Row, Henley-on-Thames RG9 5QS

www.cursillo.org.uk

Contact: Mr Stephen Fox, National Secretary

Tel: 01491 681646
E-mail: stephen.fox@cursillo.org.uk

Details: Cursillo is a Catholic movement to form leaders, who grow through prayer, study and action to evangelise others for Christ.

The movement is active in the Diocese of Clifton, and elsewhere. Three-day weekends are run on a Diocesan basis.

Focolare Movement

62 Kings Avenue, London SW4 8BH
www.focolare.org

Contact: Pat Whitney, Communications Assistant

Tel: 0208 671 8355
E-mail: pat@focolare.demon.co.uk

Details: Focolare is an international movement started by Chiara Lubich in Trent, Italy in 1943. Its principal aim is to contribute to the fulfilment of Jesus' prayer, "May they all be one". It is at the service of dialogue within and between churches, with people of different faiths and with those who want to work for peace and unity in all spheres of society. The young people's section, known as Youth for a United World, organises activities in many towns in Welwyn Garden City, as well as elsewhere.

Grandpont House

Folly Bridge, Oxford OX1 4LD
www.grandpont-house.org

Contact: Mr Jim Mirabal MA (Oxon), Director

Tel: 01865 244150
E-mail: grandponthouse@clara.co.uk

Details: Located near the centre of Oxford, Grandpont House offers accommodation to a small number of male students. It organises conferences and cultural activities, and groups of volunteers for UK and overseas social projects. Weekly guided prayer, talks and seminars given by resident chaplain; spiritual direction, days of recollection and retreats also offered. Open to people of all faiths and none. All spiritual activities are entrusted to the Opus Dei prelature.

Neocatechumenal Way, Bedford

Contact: Franco and Angela Verdura

Tel: 01234 308387
E-mail: f.verdura@ntlworld.com

Details: The Neocatechumenal Way is an itinerary of Catholic formation which, lived in small communities within the parish, helps people to rediscover and to live the immense riches of their baptism. After an initial set of teachings on the Catholic faith, those who wish to do so will form and continue as a community which then meets on a regular basis to celebrate together the Liturgy of the Word and the Eucharist, going through various stages similar to those of the 'catechumenate' of the Early Church. The Neocatechumenal Way is governed by a Statute approved by the Holy See.

Northampton Youth Ministry Office

Northampton Youth Ministry Office, Ker Anna Centre, Princes Risborough, Bucks HP27 0JN
www.nymo.org

Contact: Mr Brin Dunsire, Communications Officer

Tel: 01844 273337
E-mail: info@nymo.org

Details: Contact with youth and young adult groups in our parishes. Contact with chaplains, etc. in our schools. Information about the life of the diocese. A huge range of Catholic information and resources via our website and at our offices. Possibility of Gap-Year Mission-Team opportunities.

Oasis Prayer Meetings – 'Oases'

S.E.N.T., Sawyers Hall Lane, Brentwood, Essex CM15 9BX
www.oases.org.uk

Contact: Alice Hall and Marianna Baccelliere, Co-ordinators

Tel: 01277 215011
E-mail: info@oases.org.uk

Details: Our vision: 'turning dry ground into springs of water' (Is 41:18b–20) – to refresh, to revive, to make ready!

The Oases are growing communities of young people responding to God's call to radical faith; through this prayer network we are inspiring, equipping and motivating our generation to become the saints of the new millennium! Oasis prayer meetings take place in Taunton and Bedford, as well as elsewhere. Each Oasis community meets monthly and contains the four core elements: Fellowship, Adoration, Intercession, and Praise and Worship.

Southwark Catholic Youth Service

St Vincent's Centre, Castle Road,
Whitstable, Kent CT5 2DY
www.scys.org.uk

Contact: The Director, Manager of Staff
and Residential Centre

Tel: 01227 272900
E-mail: scys@scys.org.uk

Details: Mailing of our "Footnotes"
magazine, information with regard to
events, volunteering opportunities and a
residential youth centre that can
accommodate groups of up to 50 people
(based at Whitstable, Kent).

St John's Catholic Cathedral, Portsmouth

Bishop's House, Edinburgh Row,
Portsmouth PO1 3HG

Contact: Cathedral Dean

Tel: 02392 826170
E-mail: stjcath@portsmouth.dio.org.uk

Details: Sunday and weekday mass.
Cathedral Discovery Centre – coffee,
books, cards and resources.

Winton

4 Canterbury Road, Oxford OX2 6LU

Contact: Lesley Hickson, Director

Tel: 01865 513410
E-mail: winton4@talk21.com

Details: Opportunity for women to
further their knowledge of the Catholic
Church through provision of seminars,
conferences and a lending library. Chance
to share time and skills with
disadvantaged children throughout the
year in social improvement projects in
Oxford and abroad. Study and common
room facilities for making and sharing
friendship. The pastoral care and activities
in Winton are entrusted to the Opus Dei
Prelature.

South West: Chaplaincies

Bath University, Bath Spa University College

Ss Peter and Paul, 112 Entry Hill, Combe Down, Bath BA2 5LS
www.bath-catholics.org.uk

Contact: Rev Bill M McLoughlin OSM, Chaplain

Tel: 01225 832096   **E-mail:** fatherbill@mcloughlin.fsnet.co.uk

Details: Catholic Chaplaincy House, 5 Harley Street. At the University of Bath – Ecumenical chaplaincy building, on campus (down the steps from the library). At Bath Spa University College – no chaplaincy office, but by arranged venues.

A Catholic chaplaincy flyer is produced and available directly from the Catholic chaplain, the Ecumenical chaplaincy building at the University of Bath Campus and at the BSUC campuses at Newton St. Loe and Sion Hill. Includes information on Mass times in local churches and at the University/College (12pm on Sundays in the ecumenical chaplaincy building and at 6:30pm in St. John's, South Parade – followed by drinks and chat). It also contains information on weekends away, confession and confirmation (by appointment), Society of St Vincent de Paul and the Catholic Society. Also lists each term's events, such as guest lecturers, ecumenical prayer meetings, Taizé prayer meetings, healing Masses with exposition, Ceilidhs, pilgrimages and other liturgical events. Altar servers, musicians, readers and eucharistic ministers welcome!

Accommodation: On application to Catholic chaplain.

Bristol University

University Catholic Chaplaincy, 103 Queen's Road, Clifton, Bristol BS8 1LL
www.bris.ac.uk/depts/union/cassoc

Contact: Rev Robert King, Chaplain

Tel: 0117 914 0003

E-mail: Robert.King@bristol.ac.uk

Details: Bristol University Catholic Chaplaincy is housed in a Georgian building next to the Student Union. Facilities include a chapel, meeting rooms, a library, a bar and club room, a computer room with internet access.

Mass celebrated at 6pm on Sundays during term time. This is followed with drinks and a hot supper in the chaplaincy bar with a Catholic Society event. Mass is also celebrated on Wednesday and Thursday. The Blessed Sacrament is exposed for an hour each Tuesday. The Chaplaincy also boasts a programme of guest speakers and various social events. See website for more details.

Accommodation: The Chaplaincy can accommodate 11 students. Bathroom facilities are shared as is the washing machine and drying room. There is a well-equipped kitchen and dining room, with a room for preparing an evening meal four times a week. Resident students also enjoy the use of the library, computer room and common room (with TV and video).

College of St Mark and St John

www.marjon.ac.uk/support/chaplaincy/

Details: For details of the provision for Catholic Chaplaincy, please approach the College.

Exeter University

Boniface House, Glenthorne Road, Exeter EX4 4QU
gosh.ex.ac.uk/societies/catholic/index.html

Contact: Rev Paul Cummins, Chaplain

Tel: 01392 271191

E-mail: p.m.cummins@exeter.ac.uk

Details: The Chaplain is present to encourage and to support the Christian life of the students and staff of the university: by leading worship, by trying to live a Christian life himself, by being around the place and available generally, by being someone who will take time to listen to you if you want to talk something through, and by being in contact with all sorts of people, both within and outside the campus. Mass takes place twice a week at the Catholic Chaplaincy, Boniface House: Sunday morning at 11.30am and Wednesday evening at 7.30pm.

Gloucester, University College

www.glos.ac.uk/uogabout/content.asp?rid=12

Details: For details of the provision for Catholic chaplaincy, please approach the College. The College as an institution seeks to be both Christian and inclusive.

University of Plymouth

Christ the King Presbytery, Armada Way, Plymouth PL1 2EN

Contact: Sr Marion Gormley, Chaplain

Tel: 01752 266523

E-mail: m.gormley@plymouth.ac.uk

Details: Attached to city-centre church on the Hoe (sea front). Large hall available.

Sunday evening Mass followed by supper. Walks on Dartmoor with Ecumenical Chaplaincy. Monthly Taizé Prayer. Monthly bowling nights with Ecumenical Chaplaincy. Other seasonal social events.

Accommodation: Four bedrooms, shared kitchen and lounge, and use of guest room when available.

. . . .

University of Portsmouth

Catholic Chaplaincy, 22A Cottage Grove, Southsea, Hants PO5 1EN
www.port.ac.uk/departments/chaplaincy/faiths/christianity/catholic.htm

Contact: Sr Marguerite Wong FMDM

Tel: 023 9283 2905
E-mail: marguerite.wong@port.ac.uk

Details: The Catholic chaplaincy is available to students at 22A Cottage Grove, weekday evenings and weekends. There is an ecumenical chaplaincy meeting room on the Guildhall campus at the Nuffield Centre (Room 2:12). Free tea/coffee available. Open 9am – 5pm, Mon – Thurs, and 9am – 4pm, Friday.

Sharing faith, food and friendship, via prayer and Bible study groups; Sunday lunch every two weeks; Sunday supper and video alternates with the above; and a listening ear plus tea/coffee, etc. Students are encouraged to attend Mass at the nearest local parish. For Mass times in the area, leaflets are available from both the ecumenical chaplaincy and the Catholic chaplaincy. Details for the University of Portsmouth Catholic society are available at: www.port.ac.uk/departments/chaplaincy/cathsoc/

University of West of England

The Octagon Ecumenical Chaplaincy Centre, University of the West of England, Frenchay Campus, Cold Harbour Lane, Bristol BS16 1QY
www.uwe.ac.uk/cathsoc

Contact: Rev Bob Rainbow AMIMechE, Chaplain

Tel: 0117 344 2334
E-mail: Robert.Rainbow@uwe.ac.uk

Details: The Chaplaincy centre at Frenchay Campus, just outside the Bolland Library. Large lounge open 8am to mid evening, quiet room, spiritual library and committee room. Chaplain's and secretary's offices, kitchenette, toilets all fully wheelchair-friendly.

Full-time on-site Catholic priest-chaplain. Mass: Frenchay Campus – Thurs 12.30pm at the octagon Quiet Room. Glenside Campus – Tues 12.30pm at the chaplain's room. Sunday – lifts available from Frenchay Campus to St Teresa's Church, Filton, on request. UWE Cathsoc Catholic students' society with a programme of social and spiritual events. Confessions and chat with chaplain (best to phone first). Preparation for sacraments. Opportunity to share in activities at the Octagon Centre and weekly chaplain's e-mail to all who apply.

South West: Organisations

Cathedral Church of St Peter and St Paul

Clifton Park, Bristol BS8 3BX
www.cliftoncathedral.org.uk

Contact: Canon Robert Corrigan, Cathedral Dean

Tel: 0117 973 8411
E-mail: cathedral@cliftondiocese.com

Details: Cathedral church of the diocese of Clifton. Daily Mass, Confessions, Exposition of the Blessed Sacrament for half an hour before each weekday mass. There are four Sunday Masses. The cathedral Choir sing at the 11am Sunday Mass, and on major feast days.

Cathedral of St Mary and St Boniface

Cathedral of St Mary and St Boniface, Wyndham Street, Plymouth PL1 5HW

Tel: 01752 662537

Details: The cathedral church of the Diocese of Plymouth.

Plymouth Diocese, Department for Formation

Cardinal Newman House, Wonford Road, Exeter EX2 4PF
www.plymouth-diocese.org.uk/

Contact: Miss Rebecca Hughes, Co-Ordinator for Youth Ministry

Tel: 01392 671324/320 **E-mail:** Rebecca@plymouth.diocesan.office.org.uk

Details: Links to key contacts and activities throughout the Diocese. A programme of short courses. Gap-year community outreach project in Efford, Plymouth – in progress, please contact Rebecca for further details.

Wales: Chaplaincies

Aberystwyth, University of Wales

Details: For details of Catholic support, please the University or local Catholic churches.

Bangor, University of Wales

Catholic Chaplaincy, 1 Menai Avenue, Bangor, Gwynedd LL57 2HH

Contact: Mrs Roberta Canning, Chaplain

Tel: 01248 352522
E-mail: RCChaplainBangor@aol.com

Details: At present the chaplaincy is in a large house close to student halls. There is a library, sitting room and meeting room and a large garden.

Social, pastoral, spiritual and intellectual support is offered. Lunches, parties, discussion, Bible study, prayer group, talks. Students go to Mass at the Catholic church which is in Upper Bangor, near the student halls. (Our Lady and St James Church, Holyhead Road, Bangor, opposite Safeway). The parish priest is responsible for the element of chaplaincy only a priest can provide. Students are of course welcome to join in parish activities.

Accommodation: There is a small flat and there are five other rooms which students can rent. We do not normally take first-year students.

Cardiff University, University of Wales Institute Cardiff, University of Wales College of Medicine, Welsh College of Music and Drama

University Catholic Chaplaincy, 62 Park Place, Cardiff CF10 3AS
www.cf.ac.uk/suon/catholic

Contact: Rev John Owen, Chaplain

Tel: 029 2022 9785
E-mail: r-c-chaplaincy@cf.ac.uk

Details: Two minutes from students union. Chaplaincy hall, chapel, common room, library (4000 books), TV and video room.

Mass on Sundays, 6.30pm, followed by supper. Daily Mass at 1.15pm. University Catholic Society, large membership, full range of activities. CAFOD group, Youth 2000 group, theological discussion group. Visiting speakers such as, Cardinal Francis Arinze, Fr G J Hughes SJ, Fr Henry Wansborough OSB, and Fr Ian Ker. Chaplain always available.

Glamorgan, University of Wales

www.glam.ac.uk/student/Chaplaincy/chap-home.php

Details: The ecumenical Chaplaincy Centre is located at 20 Llantwit Road, close to the main University entrance. The centre includes a lounge, kitchen, library, chapel and office. For details of the provision for Catholic chaplaincy, please approach the University.

Lampeter, University of Wales

Carmel RC Church, Pontfaen Road, Lampeter, Ceredigion SA48 7DS

Contact: Rev Jason A Jones, Chaplain

Tel: 01570 422437
E-mail: frjason@teilo.fsnet.co.uk

Details: Chaplaincy building is the parish priest's house. Downstairs social lounge, video/TV, kitchen. Parish church attached to house.

1st Sunday of month: student lunch. Wednesday 7pm, Mass followed by social. Lent/Advent day of recollection. Music group and Altar serving. The parish church is also the chaplaincy. The parish is small and rural. The town is predominantly Welsh-speaking. Mass is in English, Latin and Welsh. There is also a Polish community with a regular Polish Mass. Much of the activity depends on the students – prayer groups, vigils and pilgrimages have all been organised in the past. The chaplain is a 32-year-old parish priest who appreciates other young, orthodox Catholic students.

Accommodation: At present none to offer, but there is a guest room for visits to the university.

North-East Wales Institute of Higher Education

www.newi.ac.uk/studying_at_newi/Help_for_Students/Religion/Religion.htm

Details: NEWI employs an interdenominational chaplain who co-ordinates the religious activity. The Chaplain is based in the library. For details of specifically Catholic support, approach also the Cathedral Church Of Our Lady Of Sorrows, Regent Street, Wrexham, or other local Catholic churches.

Swansea, University of Wales

members.lycos.co.uk/uwschapel/index.php

Details: The ecumenical Chaplaincy is based on the ground floor of Fulton House. For details of the Catholic chaplaincy provision, please approach the University.

Wales: Organisations

Cathedral of Our Lady of Sorrows

Cathedral of Our Lady of Sorrows, Regent Street, Wrexham

Tel: 01978 263943

Details: The cathedral church of the Diocese of Wrexham.

St David's Cathedral

St David's Cathedral, Charles Street, Cardiff

Tel: 029 2023 1407

Details: The cathedral church for the Archdiocese of Cardiff.

St Joseph's Cathedral

St Joseph's Cathedral, Convent Street, Swansea SA1 2BX

Tel: 01792 652683

Details: The cathedral church for the Diocese of Menevia.

Chaplaincies for International Students

African Chaplaincy in Britain

St George's Presbytery, 132 Shernall Street, Walthamstow, London E17 9HU

Contact: Rev Joseph Baffour-Awuah, National Director

Tel: 0208 521 2359 **E-mail:** joseph.baffour.awuah@barnfield.ac.uk

Details: The Chaplaincy is attached to St George's Catholic Church. Facilities include the use of parish church, hall and meeting room.

The Chaplaincy arranges African Liturgies, cultural activities, annual retreat, pilgrimage, discussion and other appropriate gatherings; annual African Mass, monthly mass and social by various African Community Associations; weekly Catholic charismatic prayer group meeting; provision of spiritual support and pastoral care for students. African Clergy freely available. Encouragement given to various African Catholics, especially students and lapsed Catholics, to establish regular contact with their parishes.

Accommodation: The Chaplaincy helps students to get accommodation by referring them to their national community associations and appropriate agencies.

Filipino Students in the UK

Filipino Missions, St Mary's, 8 Clapham Park Road, London SW4 7AP

Contact: Rev Claro V Conde CSsR, Chaplain

Tel: 0207 627 1386
E-mail: cconde8254@aol.com

Details: Serving Ethnic Filipino students in the UK. Orientation and integration into British life. Introduction to Filipino student groups/network. Counselling and Spiritual direction. Filipino liturgical celebrations.

Accommodation: Host Filipino families in the UK.

Lebanese Maronite Order

6 Dobson Close, Swiss Cottage, London NW6 4RS
www.maronitechurch.co.uk

Contact: Rev Augustine Aoun, Chaplain

Tel: 0207 586 1801
E-mail: AAAoun@aol.com

Details: Serves Lebanese Maronite Order.

Scalabrini Centre

Scalabrini Centre, 20 Brixton Road, London SW8 6BU

Contact: Rev Pietro Gelotto, Chaplain

Tel: 0207 735 8235
E-mail: padrepietro@scalabrini.co.uk

Details: Chiesa del Redentore; Italian Catholic Mission. Masses: Sunday 10.30am–12pm, Mon–Fri 7.30pm, Sat 7pm. Social and entertaining initiatives.

Accommodation: Casa della Studente, 174–176 Clapham Road, London SW8 0LA – accommodation for young women.

St Casimir's Lithuanian Church

21 The Oval, London E2 9DT
www.londonas.co.uk

Contact: Rev Petras Tverijonas, Chaplain

Tel: 0207 739 8735
E-mail: ptverijonas@btinternet.com

Details: Church, small library, meeting rooms.

Lithuanian St Casimir's Church. Sunday Masses at 9am, 11am and 6pm. 7pm discussion group.

Velehrad

Velehrad, 22 Ladbroke Square, London W11 3NA

Contact: Rev John Lang SJ, Chaplain

Tel: 0207 727 7849
E-mail: velehrad@btconnect.com

Details: 5 minutes from Notting Hill Gate tube station. There is a library, chapel, meeting room with kitchen and a small garden.

Velehrad is a Catholic centre where people meet to talk, to discuss, to spend a little time together.

Accommodation is offered for those from the Czech and Slovak Republic. Mass is held each day and confessions can be heard daily. You can also go to Mass at 114 Mount Street, Mayfair (Bond Street tube) at 10.30am every Sunday. If you can sing or play any musical instrument you are welcome to join our choir. After the main Mass we meet for coffee and a chat.

Accommodation: Single room £10/night. Double room £8/night per person. Three- or four-person room £7/night per person. Max stay 1 month (only open to Czech and Slovak people).

Vietnamese Pastoral Centre

The Vietnamese Pastoral Centre, 10–12 Wye Cliff Road, Handsworth, Birmingham B20 3TB
www.vietmartyrs.org.uk

Contact: Rev Peter Nguyen Tien Dac, Chaplain

Tel: 0121 554 8082

Details: The pastoral centre has a Chapel, a Marian Shrine and several meeting rooms.

The pastoral centre serves the Vietnamese Catholics living in Birmingham and the surrounding areas. Sacraments are celebrated in Vietnamese. There are various activities to help the Vietnamese Catholics preserve their cultural heritage and integrate into our society.

National Listings

Catholic Education

Gap Years

Organisations

Internet Resources

Catholic Education

Catholic Bible School

Nutbourne House, Farm Lane, Nutbourne, Chichester, W.Sussex PO18 8SD
www.catholic-bible-school.org

Contact: Geoff and Gina Poulter, Directors

Tel: 01243 371766

E-mail: info@catholic-bible-school.org

Details: Founded in 1988, the Catholic Bible School is an educational charitable trust which provides individuals and small groups with the opportunity to become more familiar with the Scriptures through in-house, non-residential tuition and distance learning courses. The school attracts leading scholars and theologians to speak at the regular Saturday Sudy Days. A wide variety of Distance Learning Programmes are available that are suitable for group or individual use. Specially written and produced by us, the Programme option comprise of a set of audio tapes and booklets and either a workbook or Bible commentary. Training provision is provided in modules which are designed to offer maximum flexibility to allow students to progress at their own pace.

Digby Stuart College

Digby Stuart College, University of Surrey, Roehampton Lane, London SW15 5PH

Details: See website
www.roehampton.ac.uk

Greyfriars

Greyfriars, Iffley Road, Oxford OX4 1SB

Contact: Rev Thomas Weinandy, Warden

Tel: 01865 243694 **E-mail:**
thomas.weinandy@greyfriars.ox.ac.uk

Details: Greyfriars is a small Catholic college attached to the University of Oxford. It is run by the Capuchin Franciscans. We take undergraduates and graduates of all denominations to read primarily arts. We have a chapel and library and can accommodate 16 of our own students.

Heythrop College, University of London

Kensington Square, London W8 5HQ
www.heythrop.ac.uk

Contact: Mrs Rosalie Bolland, Assistant Registrar

Tel: 0207 795 6600

E-mail: enquiries@heythrop.ac.uk

Details: As one of the smaller institutions of the University of London, Heythrop College offers degrees in philosophy and theology at undergraduate, postgraduate and doctoral levels. It also offers a non-accredited certificate programme in evangelisation and catechesis for parish ministry. Heythrop has one of the most important theological collections in the country, as well as one of the largest philosophical libraries in the University of London. The College is easily accessible from all mainline stations and has excellent underground links. It prides itself on its warm, friendly atmosphere and individual attention to students in one-to-one tutorials.

Margaret Beaufort Institute of Theology, Cambridge

Margaret Beaufort Institute of Theology, 12 Grange Road, Cambridge CB3 9DX
www.margaretbeaufort.cam.ac.uk

Contact: Dr Clare Watkins, Vice Principal

Tel: 01223 741 040 (direct), 01223 741039 (office)

E-mail: clare@drwatkins.co.uk

Details: A place of study, prayer and formation, in a Catholic theological setting. A number of part-time and full-time courses can be accessed through the institute, including Cambridge University BTh (theology for ministry), and other university-accredited qualifications in pastoral theology. We also assist sabbatical and independent-learning students in this area. Accommodation available.

Maryvale Institute

Maryvale House, Old Oscott Hill, Birmingham B44 9AG
www.maryvale.ac.uk

Contact: Mr Graham Wildsmith, Academic Registrar

Tel: 0121 360 8118

E-mail: registry.maryvale@dial.pipex.com

Details: A full range of distance-learning courses, from certificates to degree and research level, in Catholic theology, catechetics and R.E. Students include clergy, religious and lay people living in Britain and abroad. Maryvale has a reputation for excellent student support, provided by its residential sessions, its supported distance-learning units, and its approach to flexible, personal tutoring. Its programmes are characterised by academic rigour and a commitment to dynamic orthodoxy. Attention is given to fostering students' faith as well as their academic abilities. Its degree courses are validated by the Open University and by the Pontifical University, Maynooth.

Missionary Institute London

Holcome House, The Ridgeway, London NW7 4HY
www.the-mil.org.uk

Contact: Rev Renzo Marcolongo, Secretary/Registrar

Tel: 0208 906 1893

E-mail: mil@mdx.ac.uk

Details: Study of theology in a missionary context, reflection and renewal for those already engaged in pastoral work. Preparation for various types of Christian ministry, both ordained and lay.

Newman College of Higher Education

Gunners Lane, Bartley Green,
Birmingham B32 3NT

Contact: Ms Pamela Taylor, Principal

Tel: 0121 476 1181
E-mail: p.t.taylor@newman.ac.uk

Details: A range of teacher education degrees (BA, BEd) to teach in Catholic and other schools. Joint honours degrees (combination of subjects) BA/BSc. Part-time degrees in Early Years (BA) or Voluntary and Community Sector Management (BA or FdA). MA Theology. Catholic Certificate in Religious Studies. The college offers excellent student support including Chaplaincy, a choir (participating in the Church Colleges Choir Festival), volunteer opportunities with SVP and other organisations, counselling and spiritual guidance. There are also opportunities for exchange with universities in Europe including many prestigious Catholic Higher Education Institutes.

Ogilvie Institute

16 Huntley Street, Aberdeen AB10 1SH
www.ogilvie.ac.uk

Contact: Rev Tony Schmitz, Director

Tel: 01224 638 675
E-mail: director@ogilvie.ac.uk

Details: Distance-learning courses in Catholic catechesis and theology.

Plater College

Pullens Lane, Headington, Oxford OX3 0DT

Contact: Mrs Monica Dolton, Admission Officer

Tel: 01865 740500
E-mail: reception@plater.ac.uk

Details: To provide a second chance for people with few qualifications and of any age to return to full-time education. To offer this education in a Catholic College against the background of the social teaching of the Church. To provide an opportunity for people to experience residential learning. To enable students to gain qualifications and, if they wish, to proceed to further studies at University. To produce people who seek to Christianise contemporary society. 'To restore all things in Christ.' (See also entry under South East: Chaplaincies'.)

St Mary's College

Waldegrave Road, Twickenham,
Middlesex TW1 4SX
www.smuc.ac.uk

Tel: 0208 240 4000

Details: St Mary's is the oldest Catholic College in the country. With over 2,500 students on a single self-contained campus, it is easy to get to know staff and fellow students. St Mary's friendly and caring atmosphere and our excellent academic record contribute to its unique personality. It is a great place to live and study for your chosen qualification, and our excellent track record of placing our graduates in good employment or appropriate postgraduate study means that St Mary's is the right choice for many people. (See also the entry for St Mary's under Greater London: Chaplaincies).

Trinity and All Saints College

Brownberrie Lane, Horsforth,
Leeds L518 5HD
www.tasc.ac.uk

Contact: Ms Kate Molloy, Head of Admissions and Marketing

Tel: 0113 2837 100
E-mail: K-Molloy@tasc.ac.uk

Details: Undergraduate and postgraduate courses in Higher Education, including teacher-training, professional and academic subjects. For full details, see website or telephone for a prospectus. (See also the entry for Trinity and All Saints under North: Chaplaincies).

Gap Years

· · · · · · · · · · · · · · ·

Alton Castle

Alton Castle, Alton, Staffordshire ST10 4TT
www.altoncastle.co.uk

Contact: Rev John Nolan, Director

Tel: 01538 703224

E-mail: john@altoncastle.co.uk

Details: A venue for retreats, Alton castle is a neo-gothic castle overlooking the Churnet Valley. We work mostly with children aged 9–14. The Castle runs courses aimed at their pastoral, social and spiritual development. Each year we seek gap-year students to work at our castle.

· · · · · · · · · · · · · · ·

Apostleship of the Sea

Herald House, Lamb's Passage,
Bunhill Row, London EC1Y 8LE
www.stellamaris.net

Contact: John Green, Assistant Director – Fundraising

Tel: 020 7588 8285   **E-mail:** johngreen@apostleshipofthesea.org.uk

Details: *Evangelisation:* Interested in Lay Mission? AOS has lay chaplains in ports around England and Wales, as part of a dynamic mission outreach of the Church to international seafarers. Seafarers come predominantly from poor countries and face isolation, danger and even abuse and exploitation as they deliver 95% of world trade. Want to find out more? Think you may be called to a lay missionary vocation? – Get in touch.

Fundraising: You've probably never seen an international seafarer. Yet we rely on them to deliver 95% of world trade. In their work, Seafarers face isolation, danger and even abuse and exploitation. Most come from poor countries and work on 9-month or even 12-month contracts away from home. Seafarers are an invisible labour force. If you believe in justice and fair trade, why not do a charity challenge for AOS in your Gap Year?

Assumption Lay Volunteer Programme

23 Kensington Square, London W8 5HN

Contact: Caroline Burns, Lay Volunteer Co-ordinator

Tel: 0207 361 4752

E-mail: cburns@rayouth.freeserve.co.uk

Details: The Assumption Lay Volunteer Programme, which is an initiative of the Religious of the Assumption, is for those whose faith calls them to share in the lives of the poor, the young and the marginalized. The programme is designed for anyone above the age of 20 who is willing to give a minimum of one year to the service of others. Volunteers use their gifts and talents to help live out the Gospel values of love, justice and service to help build up the human family across cultural, national and other divides. ALVP is an experience of mutual giving, receiving and self-discovery. 'Everyone has a mission here on earth.' (Marie Eugenie Milleret, foundress of the Religious of the Assumption)

ATD Fourth World

48 Addington Square, London SE5 7LB
www.atd-uk.org

Contact: Beatriz Monte-Baron, Full-time Volunteer

Tel: 0207 703 3231

E-mail: atd@atd-uk.org

Details: ATD Fourth World is a human rights organisation taking an holistic approach to poverty eradication. We believe that only by working in partnership with those experiencing poverty and social exclusion can real and effective change come about in the lives of those most disadvantaged. We offer the following. Family support: encouraging families to make links with local initiatives and equipping them with the strength and confidence to work in partnership with professionals. Policy Development Programme: to enable people living in poverty to contribute to local and national policy development through building up a dialogue with policy makers. Awareness-raising: creating a network of volunteers; promoting 17 October as International Day for Eradication of Poverty; publications. Opportunities with ATD Fourth World can be on a volunteering basis or a three-month induction programme with views to a two-year commitment as a full-time volunteer.

Castlerigg Manor Youth Centre

Castlerigg Manor, Manor Brow,
Keswick CA12 4AR
www.castleriggmanor.com

Contact: Rev Paul Embery, Directory Chaplain

Tel: 01768 772711

E-mail: castleriggmanor@hotmail.com

Details: A Catholic residential youth centre in the heart of the Lake District. Available for group accommodation (self-catering/full board). Employment opportunities for age 21+ or gap year age 18+.

Catholic Network of Volunteer Service

1410 Q Street NW, Washington,
USA, DC 20009
www.cnvs.org

Contact: Recruitment Coordinator

Tel: 001 202 332 6000

E-mail: volunteer@cnvs.org

Details: CNVS offers the ability to live out the Gospel call to service by connecting full-time volunteer programmes with Christian faith-based programs. There are over 230 programmes that place volunteers in full-time (30+ hours per week) positions. Volunteer activities range from soup kitchens and social service work, to legal advocacy and medical volunteers, to computer and accounting, to agriculture and much more.

Programmes range in length from one week to several years. Programmes offer volunteer opportunities in all 50 US States, as well as in over 110 countries. Many programmes accept international volunteers who can secure their own visas. Some programmes can offer assistance in securing a visa. For more information, visit our website at www.cnvs.org and view the online Response Directory; or write to or call our office to request a free copy of the Response Directory, which describes and indexes all 230+ programmes.

Catholic Parliamentary Internships

c/o Catholic Bishops' Conference of England and Wales, 39 Eccleston Square, London SW1V 1BX
www.catholic-ew.org.uk/internships

Contact: Miss Suzanne McDougall, Programme Administrator

Tel: 0207 901 4816
E-mail: cpi@cbcew.org.uk

Details: Catholic Parliamentary Internships (CPI) is a new programme, beginning in Autumn 2003, which provides three newly graduated young Catholics with an intensive experience of political and social action. The internships run for ten months from October to July and have been established to encourage future Catholic leaders to fulfil their Christian calling in public life. The core elements of the programme are: working with a Christian MP; MA-level classes at Heythrop College, University of London (Christian Ethics and Catholic Social Teaching); visits to institutions abroad including the Vatican and EU offices in Brussels; regular spiritual guidance and an eight-day retreat.

Céilí Naomh Phádraig (Ceili Community)

Ceili Community, Ave Maria House, Ballyhaunis Road, Knock, Co Mayo, Ireland
www.ceilicommunity.net

Contact: Mgr Pat Lynch, Director

Tel: 00353 (0)94 88082
E-mail: admin@ceilicommunity.net

Details: The Ceili Community offers the possibility of becoming part of a team running missions in Primary and Secondary schools thoughout Ireland. If you are looking for ways to use your creative skill and are passionate about sharing the Gospel message in relevant and effective ways for the groups you meet, this could be for you.

Christians Abroad

Room 233, Bon Marche Centre, 241 Ferndale Road, London SW9 8BJ
www.cabroad.org.uk ; www.wse.org.uk

Contact: Mr Philip Wetherell, Recruitment

Tel: 0870 770 7990 **E-mail:** director@cabroad ; wse@cabroad.org.uk

Details: Christians Abroad recruits volunteers and skilled professionals for mission and development work, provides careers advice and support services (health insurance, briefing and debriefing, etc.) to individuals and organisations. 'World Service Enquiry' is part of Christians Abroad. It publishes an annual guide for volunteers in development and mission, a monthly overseas job list, and a unique e-mail coaching course, E>volve. 'Practicalities' is a new e-book which helps people in the practical steps of moving to a new culture as a volunteer or a worker.

Columban Lay Missionary Programme

28 Redington Road, London, NW3 7RH

Contact: Rev Frank Regan SSC, Member of Lay Missionary Team

Tel: 020 7794 8131 **E-mail:** FrEgan@Columban.freeserve.co.uk

Details:

This programme offers a three-year experience of mission abroad, discernment accompaniment, a five-month preparation course (plus language school) and – a challenge!

Craig Lodge Trust

Craig Lodge, Family House of Prayer, Dalmally, Argyll PA33 1AR

Contact: Maureen Callaghan, Manager

Tel: 01838 200216
E-mail: mail@craiglodge.org

Details: Opportunities offered: to come and experience community life for one year; to take time to discern what God is calling the individual to; to join in the community prayer life. Outreaches are: running a retreat house, evangelising to the youth in schools, helping raise awareness of over 300 million starving children in the world and, when appropriate, visiting a Third World country (this is only at the discretion of the community). It is a time of healing for the individual, a time to discover oneself, to discover the gifts that God has given and, through the community, nurturing and developing these gifts.

Friends of the Church in China

Inter-Church House, 35–41 Lower Marsh, London SE1 7RL
www.thefcc.org

Contact: China Officer

Details: Twice-yearly newsletter, website and biennial conference with information about China and its churches and about opportunities to meet Chinese students or to teach in China.

Jesuit Volunteer Community: Britain

23 New Mount Street, Manchester M4 4DE
www.jesuitvolunteers-uk.org

Contacts: Rachel Saum, Kate Goodrich

Tel: 0161 832 6888
E-mail: staff@jvc.u-net.com

Details: Provide fully-funded year and summer volunteering opportunities for 17–35 year-olds, in the UK. Live in community with volunteers from around the world. Work in inner-city placements with the marginalised, e.g. homeless, refugees, adults with learning difficulties. Explore values of social justice, spirituality, community and simple living.

L' Arche

10 Briggate, Silsden, Keighley BD20 9JT
www.larche.org.uk

Contact: Mr John Peet, General Secretary

Tel: 01535 656186
E-mail: info@larche.org.uk

Details: The opportunity to share life with people with learning disabilities. L'Arche communities consist of ordinary houses where people with and without learning disabilities live a simple shared life. Communities are ecumenical and welcome people of other faiths or none. Own room + all meals provided + pocket money.

Lasallian Developing World Projects

140 Banbury Road, Oxford OX2 7BP
www.delasalle.org.uk

Contact: Br John Deeney, Director

E-mail: ldwpuk@hotmail.com

Details: Five-week educational work project (building or teaching) in the developing world. Students work as part of a team of volunteers from the UK, sharing labour with the local community to improve education. Projects take place during July–August: preparation meetings in the course of the preceding year.

Living Water Ministry

The Visitation, Taynuilt, Argyll PA35 1JQ
www.kilmoretrust.org.uk

Contact: Sarah Brown, Ministry Coordinator

Tel: 01866 822172
E-mail: livingwater@kilmoretrust.org.uk

Details: Living Water Ministry is a Catholic evangelisation team based in Scotland, aiming specifically at youth. Team members are aged between 18 and 28 and live a community life of prayer, study, ongoing formation, training and evangelisation through retreat ministry. The team travels to schools and parishes presenting the gospel as alive and relevant in ways people can relate to and enjoy. Their commitment is from August to June.

NET Ministries (National Evangelisation Teams)

110 Crusader Ave. West, West St. Paul, MN 55118, USA
www.NETusa.org

Contact: Ms Kara Horman, Recruiting Co-ordinator

Tel: 001 651 450 6833
E-mail: recruit@NETusa.org

Details: The goal of the programme: to challenge young Catholics to love Christ and embrace the life of the Church by proclaiming the Gospel of Christ through a personal witness of faith. Type of service: Volunteers serve on teams of 12 (6 men, 6 women) which travel across the US proclaiming the Gospel to youth ages 12–18 through fun, high-energy retreats incorporating large group presentations, small group discussion, music, drama, personal faith sharings and the opportunity for each retreatant to respond to Christ in prayer and/or through the Sacraments of Reconciliation and the Eucharist. Length of service: mid-August through to May. Requirements: Roman Catholic men and women aged 18–30 who have a personal faith, possess physical stamina, are cooperative, flexible, respond well to peer leadership and are able to live simply. Volunteers are required to raise US$3,000 in partnership funds prior to the start of training. (NET provides food, lodging, medical insurance, training, supervisory care and a monthly stipend.)

Northampton Youth Ministry Office

Northampton Youth Ministry Office, Ker Anna Centre, Princes Risborough, Bucks HP27 0JN
www.nymo.org

Contact: Mr Brin Dunsire, Communications Officer

Tel: 01844 273337
E-mail: info@nymo.org

Details: The office offers the possibility of Gap-Year Mission-Team opportunities. See also the entry for Northampton Youth Ministry Office under 'South East'.

Pilgrims Community

The Pilgrims Community, Presentation Convent, Chester Road, Matlock, Derbyshire DE4 3FS
www.pilgrimscommunity.com

Contact: Rev Jonathan Cotton, Director

Tel: 01624 57704

E-mail: info@pilgrimscommunity.com

Details: The community offers volunteering opportunities suitable for a gap year: training in community living, discipleship formation and youth evangelisation; working in a school mission team; service work in the local community; opportunity for a brief overseas evangelisation experience. See also the entry under 'New Movements and Evangelisation' for other opportunities.

ReachOut! Gap Year

30 Selworthy Road, Moss Side, Manchester M16 7AH
www.reachoutuk.org

Contact: Nacho Gutierrez, Gap Year Co-ordinator

Tel: 0161 224 7648

E-mail: gapyear@reachoutuk.org

Details: ReachOut Gap Year offers students aged 18 and over an opportunity to do something different to gain valuable experience before joining university or starting professional life after it. The work usually involves helping disadvantaged people overseas on a variety of projects. Some projects require specialised skills, e.g. medical or dental students in Nicaragua, agricultural or economics students in Peru. Others, on the other hand, do not require much specialisation but simply a willingness for hard work. Based on Christian principles, our organisation guarantees the university students a Catholic atmosphere and, if they wish, the possibility to deepen their Catholic Faith. At the moment, we work in the following countries: Peru, Nicaragua and Uruguay. We are expecting to work in Mexico, the Philippines and Argentina as well.

Sacred Heart Sisters Volunteer Programme

Chigwell Convent, 803 Chigwell Road, Woodford Bridge, Essex IG8 8AU

Contact: Ms Catriona Fletcher, Programme Co-ordinator

Tel: 020 8504 1624

E-mail: SSHJMVolunteers@aol.com

Details: The opportunity to work both at home and abroad with vulnerable people in the areas of education, health, community development and empowerment, in a spirit of solidarity.

Savio House Retreat Centre

Savio House, Ingersley Road, Bollington, Macclesfield SK10 5EW
www.saviohouse.org.uk

Contact: Gill McCambridge, Retreat Director

Tel: 01625 575405

E-mail: gill@saviohouse.org.uk

Details: A gap year as a volunteer youth worker in a retreat centre for young people. A placement on a youth work / social work course.

Simon Community

PO Box 1187, London NW5 4HW
www.simoncommunity.org

Contact: Marie Cafferky, Administrator

Tel: 0207 485 6639   **E-mail:** thesimoncommunity@hotmail.com

Details: The Simon Community is a volunteer community, Catholic in foundation, Christian in inspiration, open to people of all faiths and none. Since 1963 we have been living and working as a partnership with on-the-street homeless people in London. Full-time residential and part-time volunteers are always needed. We do street-work and soup runs, and run residential houses. We also campaign on issues affecting homeless people.

Society of Our Lady of the Most Holy Trinity

St. Mary Magdalen Church, 73 Comerford Road, London SE4 2BA
www.solt3.org

Contact: Rev Morty O'Shea, SOLT

Tel: 0208 692 1824

E-mail: soltlondon@hotmail.com

Details: The Society of Our Lady of the Most Holy Trinity is a Society of Apostolic Life which serves the poor in ecclesial teams consisting of priests, religious and laity who share a common life. In particular we have need for anybody who has third-level experience to take a gap year teaching in our mission schools either in Belize (Central America), Texas or North Dakota. Volunteers preferably would have an undergraduate degree, but this is not essential. Neither is it necessary to have a teaching qualification – a CAN DO / WILL DO attitude suffices entirely! Details of SOLT and all its missions can be seen on our website.

Soli House

Mill Lane, Stratford upon Avon, Warwickshire CV37 6BJ
www.solihouse.org.uk

Contact: Rev Eddie Clare, Director

Tel: 01789 267011

E-mail: eddie@solihouse.org.uk

Details: Gap-year opportunities to Sixth Form leavers and graduates to live and work in a Catholic youth retreat centre, helping to run residential retreats for the 14–18 age group and school mission events for the Archdiocese of Birmingham.

St Claude School of Mission

St Patrick's Parish, 21a Soho Square,
London W1D 4NR
www.stpatricks.uk.com/

Contact: Rev Alexander Sherbrooke,
Director

Tel: 0207 437 2010
E-mail: stpatrick@info.com

Details: One year for God, for others, for
you. We invite you to commit one year of
your life to being trained to take on the
mission for the poor in the footsteps of
Christ in the context of our modern, inter-
cultural, and irreligious world. A life of
mission in the heart of London,
accompanied by solid personal, spiritual
and theological formation. This exciting
nine-month residential course can be
divided into two parts: Classroom training
(theological formation, spiritual
formation, leadership formation) and
Ground Training (how to evangelise,
growing in understanding of the human
person and his search for God, developing
skills, experiencing mission). The course
runs from October until June. For more
information, see our website. Candidates
should normally have completed their
tertiary education and be aged between
20 and 30. Please send a CV and a
personal letter of motivation.

Tamezin Placements

1 Chelsea Embankment, London SW3 4LG
www.opusdei.org

Contact: Sophia Pain, Placement
Co-Ordinator

Tel: 0207 3527494
E-mail: Tplacements@talk21.com

Details: Holiday or gap-year opportunities
for girls in voluntary or paid positions,
either in the UK or abroad. Possibilities
include: work with socially disadvantaged,
youth leadership projects, medical
assistance, teaching posts.

Links with established projects in socially
deprived areas of London, Manchester,
Oxford and Glasgow as well as various

locations abroad, such as Estonia, Kenya,
USA and Peru, all inspired by St Josemaria
Escriva, Founder of Opus Dei.

Time for God

2 Chester House, Pages Lane, Muswell Hill,
London N10 1PR
www.timeforgod.org

Contact: Elaine Hornsby and Glynes
Mewton

Tel: 0208 883 1504
E-mail: recruit@timeforgod.org

Details: Time for God provides
opportunities for 18–25 year olds to be
involved in full-time volunteer work in the
UK and overseas. Placements include
inner-city social action projects, homeless
and drug and alcohol rehabilitation
hostels, churches, youth retreat centres
etc. Volunteers receive accommodation,
food expenses, pocket money, three
training conferences and pastoral support.

Vincentian Volunteers

39 Marlsford St, Liverpool L6 6AX
www.vincentianvolunteers.org

Contact: Sr Pauline Gaughan, Director

Tel: 0151 261 0225 **E-mail:**
director@vicentvols.freeserve.co.uk

Details: Vincentian Volunteers are young
people between 18 and 30 years old who
live simply in little communities following
the inspiration of St Vincent de Paul, who
found Christ in the poor. Life, for these
volunteers, is made up of three strands;
community, prayer and service. The
commitment they make is from September
to July.

Youth Mission Team

16 Arthur Street Blyth, Northumberland
NE24 1EA
www.ymt.org

Contact: Rev Dermott Donnelly, Director

Tel: 01670 351703
E-mail: admin@ymt.org

Details: YMT is a radical youth
organisation committed to developing
youth ministry in the Church. As well as
full-time staff, volunteers come from all
over the world to develop and discover
new ways of reaching out with the Gospel.
YMT works with young people in schools,
parishes, retreats, conferences and
festivals. It is also involved working with
adults offering support, formation and
training. The development of holistic
youth activities (spiritual, justice-based,
and social) throughout the diocese is the
constant aim of YMT. YMT is also pushing
forward full-time positions for youth
ministers in local areas such as parishes,
pastoral areas and deaneries. YMT offers
places on its volunteer programme to
young people, offering them training and
experience in youth ministry with the
possibility also of qualifications.

New Movements and Evangelisation

CaFE – Catholic Faith Exploration

Catholic Evangelisation Services, PO Box 333, St Albans AL2 1EL
www.faithcafe.org

Contact: Mr David Payne, Director

Tel: 01727 822 837
E-mail: info@faithcafe.org

Details: CaFE is a video course to help Catholics get excited about their faith in a fun and relevant way. Small groups are formed to grow together and seek new ways to share the Good News with others.

Catholic Charismatic Renewal Centre

Allen Hall, 28 Beaufort Street, London SW3 5AA
www.ccr.org.uk

Contact: Mrs Kristina Cooper, Editor of *Goodnews*

Tel: 0207 352 5298
E-mail: ccruk@onetel.net.uk

Details: Contacts with prayer groups and communities in Britain and abroad. Goodnews – bi-monthly magazine with teaching on spiritual life and the charisms, news of coming events, inspirational stories of what God is doing, and evangelisation training courses.

Communion and Liberation

79 Twyford Avenue, West Acton, London W3 9QD
www.clonline.org.uk

Contact: Dr Amos Lawless

Tel: 0799 0543866
E-mail: cl_uk@onetel.net.uk

Details: The experience of Communion and Liberation is that the encounter with Christ present through a friendship is the true source of liberation and therefore the only complete answer to the deepest human desires. The method of Communion and Liberation is most of all to share and judge our daily lives, in particular through a weekly meeting called School of Community.

Cursillos in Christianity

Clayton House, Newlands Lane, Stoke Row, Henley-on-Thames RG9 5QS
www.cursillo.org.uk

Contact: Mr Stephen Fox, National Secretary

Tel: 01491 681646
E-mail: stephen.fox@cursillo.org.uk

Details: Cursillo is a Catholic course to form leaders, who grow through prayer, study and action to evangelise others for Christ.

The movement is active in the Dioceses of Birmingham, Clifton, Hallam and Liverpool. Three-day weekends are run on a Diocesan basis.

Faith Movement

9 Herma St, Cadder, GLASGOW G23 5AP
www.faith.org.uk

Contact: Ann McCallion

Tel: 0141 945 0393

Details: The Faith movement is a group of priests, religious and lay Catholics. We work together to foster the Catholic faith and spiritual life of many people, especially through youth events and various publications. In particular, there is the Summer Youth Session, for 16–30 year olds each August (five days of lectures, discussion and seminars around a particular theme, in a relaxed holiday environment, with daily Mass and prayer) and the Students Winter Conference in early January each year (three days of reflection, discussion and other activities, again with Mass and prayer).

Focolare Movement

62 Kings Avenue, London SW4 8BH
www.focolare.org

Contact: Pat Whitney, Communications Assistant

Tel: 0208 671 8355
E-mail: pat@focolare.demon.co.uk

Details: Focolare is an international movement started by Chiara Lubich in Trent, Italy in 1943. Its principal aim is to contribute to the fulfilment of Jesus' prayer, "May they all be one". It is at the service of dialogue within and between churches, with people of different faiths and with those who want to work for peace and unity in all spheres of society. The young people's section, known as Youth for a United World, organises activities in many towns in Great Britain, including London, Leeds, Liverpool, Glasgow, Edinburgh and Welwyn Garden City.

Institute for World Evangelisation (ICPE Mission)

Via della Stazione Aurelia 95, 00165 Rome, Italy
www.icpe.org

Contact: Mario Cappello, International Director

E-mail: imc@icpe.org

Details: Schools of Mission, a four-month full-time training programme where participants experience community life as well as practical formation in the area of evangelisation and Christian formation. Participants will also go for a mission outreach in a neighbouring country. Mission:/Possible, an initiative to mobilise people for long- and short-term missions in areas of great need.

Maranatha Community

102 Irlam Road, Flixton,
Manchester M41 6JT
www.maranathacommunity.org.uk

Contact: Mr M Kendrick, Warden

Tel: 0161 748 4858   **E-mail:**
office@maranathacommunity.freeserve.co.uk

Details: Maranatha is a scattered but
vibrant community of thousands of
Christians who are active in their own
churches and parishes. Catholics join with
Protestants in common witness and work.
Maranatha has generated a considerable
amount of work with the homeless,
prostitutes and drug addicts at street
level and it also has an extensive healing
ministry, bringing together a wide range
of specialist disciplines, including doctors,
educationalists, social workers and priests.
It is actively engaged in a broad range of
research projects in many areas of social
concern. It is deeply involved in
Parliamentary work and has generated
numerous overseas projects. It is equally
committed to social action and
contemplative prayer and works closely
with Christian leaders. It is committed to
work and pray for Christian unity, renewal
and healing. It arranges a full programme
of residential training courses and
retreats. The Community also produces an
extensive range of training and research
publications.

Oasis Prayer Meetings – 'Oases'

S.E.N.T., Sawyers Hall Lane, Brentwood,
Essex CM15 9BX
www.oases.org.uk

Contact: Alice Hall and Marianna
Baccelliere, Co-ordinators

Tel: 01277 215011
E-mail: info@oases.org.uk

Details: Our vision: 'turning dry ground
into springs of water' (Is 41:18b-20) – to
refresh, to revive, to make ready! The
Oases are growing communities of young
people responding to God's call to radical
faith; through this prayer network we are
inspiring, equipping and motivating our
generation to become the saints of the
new millennium! Oasis prayer meetings
take place in London, Bedford,
Birmingham and Taunton. Each Oasis
community meets monthly and contains
the four core elements: Fellowship,
Adoration, Intercession, and Praise and
Worship.

Opus Dei

www.opusdei.org

Contact: Opus Dei Information Office in
Britain

Tel: 0207 221 9176

Details: Opus Dei exists to help people
discover God through their everyday work,
study and family life. It was founded in
1928 by the Spanish priest, Josemaría
Escrivá, who was canonised (declared a
saint) by Pope John Paul II in 2002. St
Josemaría preached tirelessly that any
honest job can be a path to God. He
helped men and women students,
professionals, labourers and housewives
realise that by working well and offering
their efforts to God, they could become
great saints. Opus Dei is a personal
prelature of the Catholic Church and has
over 80,000 members worldwide. In
Britain its members run various university
residences and centres, youth clubs, and
social initiatives for disadvantaged
youngsters.

Pilgrims Community

The Pilgrims Community, Presentation
Convent, Chester Road, Matlock,
Derbyshire DE4 3FS
www.pilgrimscommunity.com

Contact: Rev Jonathan Cotton, Director

Tel: 01624 57704
E-mail: info@pilgrimscommunity.com

Details: Evangelisation retreats and
courses offered to chaplaincies, parishes
and schools. The community has a core
group of long-term and life-time members,
reflecting all vocations. See also entry
under 'Gap Years' for volunteering
opportunities.

Sion Catholic Community for Evangelism

S.E.N.T., Sawyers Hall Lane, Brentwood,
Essex CM15 9BX
www.sioncommunity.org.uk

Contact: Alice Hall, Youth Discipleship
Team leader

Tel: 01277 215011
E-mail: alice.hall@sioncommunity.org.uk

Details: Sion Community's youth
discipleship team offers a student
outreach that seeks to support groups/
societies of Christian students. We offer
training in leadership, Catholic
apologetics and evangelism. We can
provide speakers and creative
presentations for events. We are able to
work with groups on an on-going basis,
developing vision, formation in faith and
places of belonging.

Youth 2000

P.O Box 176, Leeds LS17 9XU
www.youth2000.org

Contact: Mrs Josie Callaghan, Deputy
National Leader

Tel: 01937 579700
E-mail: info@youth2000.org

Details: Youth 2000 is an international
spiritual initiative run by young people for
young people which provides a programme
of retreats and spiritual events throughout
the country. The heart of Youth 2000 is
Eucharistic adoration and Holy Scripture.
The organisation allows young people to
find friends and community who are living
their faith and to be actively involved in
taking the Gospel out to others.

Other Organisations

Across Jumbulances

52 Westermains Ave, Kirkintilloch,
Glasgow G66 1EH
www.jumbulance.co.uk

Contact: Sylvia Stark, Secretary

Tel: 0141 777 6931

E-mail: jumbulance@lineone.net

Details:

Across Jumbulances provide a ten-day pilgrimage to Lourdes for seriously ill or disabled people. Volunteer carers with or without experience are required throughout the year. Whilst all individuals pay their own fare, assistance can be given for fundraising.

Ampleforth Abbey

Hospitality & Pastoral Office,
Ampleforth Abbey, York YO62 4EN
www.ampleforth-hpo.org.uk

Contact: Jan Fitzalan Howard, Director – Hospitality

Tel: 01439 766889

E-mail: hospitality@ampleforth.org.uk
pastoral@ampleforth.org.uk

Details: Guest accommodation throughout most of the year is available for university groups or those wishing for a quiet break from a hectic term! Promoted retreats and workshops advertised on the website and mailed in programme form, again all open to students. Community welcomes guests to share the Easter Triduum: School Houses are opened especially for the four days.

CAFOD

CAFOD, Romero Close, London SW9 9TY
www.cafod.org.uk

Contact: Mr Ged Naughton, Youth Team Leader

Tel: 0207 326 5685

E-mail: youth@cafod.org.uk

Details: CAFOD works in England and Wales with young people of school and higher-education age. We encourage young people to reflect on their own position in a global context and take action for change. We work through 12 regional offices around the country and in partnership with People and Planet, who are part-funded through our Development Education Fund.

Catholic Unattached Directory

118 Shepherds Lane, Dartford DA1 2NN
www.cathud.com

Contact: Mr Graham Moorhouse, Membership Secretary

Tel: 01322 222213

E-mail: help@cathud.com

Details: The unattached directory is run by practising Catholics for practising Catholics. It is a modern fun way to make new friends and even meet that someone special.

Catholic Union of Great Britain

St Maximilian Kolbe House,
63 Joddo Road, London W12 9EE
www.catholicunion.org

Contact: Mr Peter Higgs, Hon. Secretary

Tel: 0208 735 0816

E-mail: hhiggs@carthanion.fsnet.co.uk

Details: Represents Catholics in public life and especially in parliamentary affairs. Those interested in Catholic Social Teaching could get to know the life of Parliament and assist Peers, MPs and MEPs. The CUGB is a voluntary lay body with no party political affiliations, that is a Catholic voice in public life. Work with Peers, MPs and MEPs by helping to make briefings or submissions to Parliamentary and other bodies. Subscription is £10 for under 25s. Visit our website!

Family Publications

6a King Street, Jericho, Oxford OX2 6DF
www.familypublications.co.uk

Contact: Richard Brown, Editor

Tel: 01865 558336

E-mail: sales@familypublications.co.uk

Details: Family Publications, the publisher of the *Catholic Student Guide*, publishes and distributes Catholic books and videos with a special focus on the needs of the Catholic population in this country, including young adults. FP also organises conferences on contemporary issues for Catholics.

Guild of Catholic Doctors

The Secretariat, Brampton House,
Hospital of St John & St Elizabeth,
60 Grove End Road, London NW8 9NH
www.catholicdoctors.org.uk

Contact: Dr J H M Morewood, Honorary Secretary

Tel: 0207 266 4246

Details: The Guild has a network of branches throughout England and Wales which have regular meetings. Ethical and medico-ethical advice is freely available and membership of the Guild is open to medical students at the reduced rate of £2 per annum. The Guild publication, *The Catholic Medical Quarterly*, contains a variety of articles on medical and ethical issues together with book reviews and comment upon relevant newspaper articles and parliamentary debates of medical significance.

The Guild holds an annual symposium at a different venue each year. Medical students wishing to attend will be welcomed and accommodation costs, etc., are heavily subsidised by the Guild branches.

HCPT: The Pilgrimage Trust

Oakfield Park, 32 Bilton Rd, Rugby, Warwickshire CV22 7WQ
www.hcpt.org.uk

Contact: Mr Michael Orbell, Director of Communications

Tel: 01788 564646

E-mail: hg@hcpt.org.uk

Details: HCPT takes children and adults with disabilities to the shrine of Our Lady of Lourdes. Young volunteer helpers are always welcome to assist in this work.

Linacre Centre for Healthcare Ethics

60 Grove End Road, London NW8 9NH
www.linacre.org

Contact: Mr Anthony McCarthy, Research Fellow

Tel: 0207 806 4088

E-mail: admin@linacre.org

Details: The Linacre Centre is a Catholic bioethics centre based in London. We give talks and lectures, run conferences, produce publications and give advice to health professionals and students on moral issues in healthcare and research on human beings.

Loyola Hall Spirituality Centre

Loyola Hall, Warrington Road, Rainhill, Prescott, Merseyside L35 6NZ
www.loyolahall.co.uk

Contact: Rev Paul Nicholson SJ, Director

Tel: 0151 426 4137

E-mail: loyola@clara.net

Details: The centre offers a year-round programme of individually-guided and themed retreats. All of these are open to students at a reduced rate. Each year three events target students and younger adults: a) Holy Week and Easter, celebrating the liturgies in a lively group setting or in quiet with individual guidance; b) Challenging Faith, a 10-day summer programme combining a retreat with a chance to explore theological ideas; c) In Search of a Way, a pre-Christmas retreat with workshops on prayer and decision-making for those looking at changes in their life. Other items on the programme include Beginners' Retreats (no previous experience necessary!), and Rest and Relaxation days. The team is available for individual spiritual direction, and offers guided prayer events within university chaplaincies.

National Office For Vocation

The Chase Centre, 114 West Heath Road, London NW3 7TX
www.ukpriest.org

Contact: Rev Kevin Dring, Director

Tel: 0208 458 6017   **E-mail:** vocation@nationaloffice.freeserve.co.uk

Details: The Office, part of the Bishops Conference of England and Wales, provides a national resource to promote the vocation of all members of the Church. It also offers advice and support for those discerning a possible vocation to religious life or ordained ministry.

Scottish Catholic International Aid Fund (SCIAF)

19 Park Circus, Glasgow G3 6BE
www.sciaf.org.uk

Contact: Victoria Murray, Communications Officer

Tel: 0141 354 5555

E-mail: sciaf@sciaf.org.uk

Details: SCIAF supports poor communities overseas, raises awareness of the underlying causes of poverty, and campaigns for a fairer world. It is the overseas relief and development agency of the Catholic Church in Scotland.

St Anthony Communications

Mount Carmel, St Brides Lane, Saundersfoot, Pembrokeshire SA69 9HL
www.saintant.com

Contact: Mr C Holden, Proprietor

Tel: 01834 812643

E-mail: sales@saintant.com

Details: We offer a wide range of Catholic audio tapes, CDs and books. We also run an annual conference for young Catholics aged 15–30.

Student Cross

www.studentcross.org.uk

Contact: General Organising Director

E-mail: god@studentcross.org.uk

Details: Student Cross is an annual walking pilgrimage run by and for students and recent graduates. There are nine different groups, or 'legs' of about 25–30 people each, who walk from different points across the country to meet at Walsingham in Norfolk on Good Friday to celebrate Easter together. Each group walks around 120 miles over the week, staying overnight in church halls, community centres or parishioners' homes, and they usually meet the Friday before Easter to begin walking, although there is also a 3-day leg and a 1-day leg for those unable to take a whole week off. Groups start from London, Oxford, Nottingham, Leicester, Kettering, Colchester and Ely, and the cost for students is around £40, including all food and accommodation. For those who cannot afford the whole cost however, there is also a related association called the Student Cross Association, which exists solely to provide grants to students and other unwaged pilgrims who would not be able to walk

Student Cross – otherwise please contact the General Organising Director listed above for more details. Student Cross is a very physical and powerful way of experiencing Easter, and even if you only walk one year you are guaranteed not to forget it!

Student LifeNet

Student LifeNet, PO Box 353, Potters Bar, Hertfordshire EN6 1WQ
www.studentlifenet.org.uk

Contact: Director, Director

Tel: 07765 805742
E-mail: slifenet@btinternet.com

Details: Student LifeNet is a network of prolife students coming together to defend human life and campaign for both real support for pregnant students and medical research which does not involve destroying human life. Recent events (reported internationally) include demonstrating as Tony Blair clones in London and France, wearing 'former embryo' t-shirts, and holding pictures of a 21-week-old baby. We can make a difference with your help. If you care about human rights, believe students matter, are interested in cutting-edge politics, law, science, or ethics, or want to know more, e-mail us via our website above. Pro-life societies are present at the Universities of Birmingham, Cambridge, Durham, Exeter, Kent, Leeds, Manchester, Oxford, Sheffield and St Andrews, and individuals at many more.

Young Christian Workers

YCW Office, St Joseph's, Watford Way, London NW4 4TY

Contact: Mrs Angela Davies, National President

Tel: 0208 203 6290
E-mail: AngelaatYCW@aol.com

Details: YCW is a movement which is run by young people who, by action and reflection, attempt to change and improve their lives and the wider society. YCW helps to develop the confidence, social skills, faith and social awareness of the young people it touches. YCW runs two programmes: 14–17-year-olds meet through Impact; and YCW is for 18+. Each group is organised around a parish or local area. Opportunities exist to meet other young people from all over the country through meetings, training events and social occasions.

Support Organisations

. . . .

Calix Society

51 Park Avenue, Chadderton,
Oldham OL9 0AL

Contact: Mr Thomas Head, National Secretary

Tel: 0161 624 2815

Details: To interest members of the Fellowship of Alcoholics Anonymous in the spiritual development of total abstinence. Members of AA or others interested are welcome. The recovery programme for the alcoholic is physical, psychological and spiritual. Calix builds on the AA programme and stresses spiritual recovery into contented sobriety. There are Calix units in several cities in England and Scotland.

. . . .

Cardinal Winning's Pro-life Initiative

104 Albert Road, Crosshill,
Glasgow G42 8DR
www.pro-lifeinitiative.org

Contact: Sr Roseann Reddy, Co-ordinator

Tel: 0141 433 2680

E-mail: gospeloflife@btinternet.com

Details: We offer a crisis pregnancy support service to any woman regardless of age, faith, etc. Aware that Catholic students are often involved in promoting a pro-life stance against all odds, we can provide the back-up practical care and support for any of their peers who may be faced with a crisis pregnancy.

Catholic Blind Services

PO Box 10333, Birmingham B13 8XX

Contact: Sean O'Donnell, Director

Tel: 07973 908274

Details: CBS will offer support to any student who is blind or visually impaired, pastorally, spiritually and within the professional circumstances that the student faces. CBS supports students who are keen to become volunteer helpers in its work – especially in helping other students.

. . . .

Catholic Deaf Association

Hennessy House, Sudell Street, Manchester M4 4JF
cda-uk.com

Contact: Rev Peter McDonough, Secretary

Tel: 0161 834 8828

Details: Services provided for deaf people: Pastoral work (i.e. visiting, counselling etc), Weekly Mass in sign (St Patrick's, Livesey St, Collyhurst), Monthly Masses in sign (Ashton, Blackburn, Bolton, Burnley, Oldham & Rochdale) and other religious services, i.e. Baptism. Courses for deaf people, such as CCRS (Catholic Certificate in Religious Studies). Training for pastoral workers and volunteers, deaf awareness and sign language. National Conferences, retreats, outreach magazine, training, pilgrimage to Walsingham, and more.

. . . .

EnCourage

EnCourage, PO Box 3745, London N2 8LW
www.encouragetrust.org.uk

Contact: Nigel, Newsletter Secretary

E-mail: petroc@encouragetrust.org.uk

Details: EnCourage is a spiritual support network for homosexual Catholics wishing to live according to the teaching of the Church. EnCourage meets regularly in Manchester, runs a website with links to student-relevant material, produces a newsletter and sells books.

Good Counsel Network

538 Kings Drive, Wembley, Middlesex HA9 9JD

Contact: Mrs Clare McCullough, Director

Tel: 0207 723 1740 **E-mail:** Clare@goodcounselnetwork.freeserve.co.uk

Details: We are a Catholic, pro-life organisation which offers counselling and support to women in unplanned pregnancy to enable them to choose to let their children live. Our helpline can provide advice on the Church's teaching on abortion, contraception and infertility treatment as well as the effects they have.

. . . .

LIFE

LIFE House, Newbold Terrace, Leamington Spa CV32 4EA
www.lifeuk.org

Contact: Mrs Nuala Scarisbrick, Trustee and Hon. Administrator

Tel: 01926 428157
E-mail: info@lifeuk.org

Details: Contact with local branches of LIFE, which are established in most towns with universities/colleges. Speakers for Catholic Societies. Practical help to Catholic students with relationship/pregnancy problems. Free student membership. Help with setting up and running a pro-life society in the university/college.

. . . .

National Council of the Catholic Handicapped Fellowship

15 Woodlands Park Drive, Blaydon, Tyne and Wear NE21 5PQ
www.rc.net/uk/national-chf

Contact: Mr John Mair, National Secretary

Tel: 0191 414 3221
E-mail: jmair@talk21.com

Details: An opportunity to work and socialise with young people who have physical disabilities and/or learning difficulties. Several small groups exist nationally that meet weekly and are run by volunteers. The groups would welcome additional help in running and organising their weekly meetings. Contact National Secretary or visit website for details.

Pioneer Total Abstinence Association

Pioneer Total Abstinence Association of the Sacred Heart, Handmaids of the Sacred Heart of Jesus, 25 St Edmunds Terrace, London NW8 7PY

Contact: Mrs Una O'Halloran, Youth Officer

Tel: 0207 336 8304

Details: The Young Pioneer Movement is part of a larger group known as the Pioneer Total Abstinence Association of the Sacred Heart. Members make their promises not just for their own good and safety but for the glory of the Sacred Heart of Jesus and out of love and concern for those who abuse alcohol and drugs. It is very much in keeping with Pope John Paul's message to young people: "[the world] needs you to be the salt of the earth and the light of the world" (Toronto 2002). Young pioneers are encouraged to form their own committees and organise their own spiritual and leisure activities. It is important to show that alcohol abuse is not required for enjoyment and that those who choose not to drink can lead full, happy, joyful lives.

Internet Resources

GENERAL CATHOLIC SITES

Catholic Church in England and Wales
www.catholic-ew.org.uk

Catholic Directory
Searchable directory of what's Catholic in Britain
www.catholicdirectory.org

Catholic Net
Good starting point for any Catholic search
www.catholic.net

Catholic Online
Plenty of useful links
www.catholic.org

Catholic.org.uk
An excellent place to meet and explore the Catholic Faith
www.catholic.org.uk

Catholic Pages
www.catholic-pages.com

Catholic Yellow Pages
If it's Catholic and online, it's probably here
www.monksofadoration.org/directory2.html

CatholiCity
www.catholicity.com

Cathport
The website from *The Tablet*
www.cathport.com

Catolicos
A wide range of links to other Catholic sites
www.catolicos.org

Christus Rex
Another wide range of links to sites of Catholic interest
www.christusrex.org

Praise of Glory
A beautiful site that offers a range of links, articles and quotes
www.praiseofglory.com

DOCUMENTS

Catechism of the Catholic Church
The definitive guide to the Catholic Faith
www.scborromeo.org/ccc.htm

Church Fathers
www.knight.org/advent/fathers

Documents of Vatican II
Access to all the texts from Vatican II
www.vatican.va/archive/hist_councils/ii_vatican_council/index.htm

Eternal Word Television Network (EWTN) document library
Whatever you're looking for, it's probably here
www.ewtn.com/vlibrary/search.asp

New Advent
Includes a Catholic Encyclopaedia, the Summa Theologica and the writings of Church Fathers
www.newadvent.org

Revised Standard Version Online
Easy-to-use Scripture searcher
www.hti.umich.edu/r/rsv

Writings of Pope John Paul II
Links to all the writings of John Paul II
www.vatican.va

Catholic Educators' Resource Centre
Provides access to resources for use in teaching the Catholic faith
www.newadvent.org

Catholic periodicals
catholic.net/rcc/Periodicals

CATHOLIC NEWS

Catholic Herald
www.catholicherald.co.uk

Catholic News Service
American-based, but with a global perspective
www.catholicnews.com

Catholic.org.uk news
British Catholic news
www.catholic.org.uk/news/index.shtml

EWTN news
Catholic news from around the world
www.ewtn.com/vnews/headlines.asp

Universe
www.totalcatholic.com

ZENIT Catholic News Agency
Providers of quality Catholic news
www.zenit.org

BOOKS AND PUBLISHERS

Catholic Truth Society
Publishers of official documents and booklets on faith and morals
www.cts-online.org.uk/cts.htm

Family Publications
The publishers of this Guide! Innovative Catholic book publishers, and distributors of a large variety of Catholic books and videos from a wide range of sources, including Ignatius Press.
www.familypublications.co.uk

Saint Anthony Communications
Distributors of a large selection of books and tapes.
www.saintant.com

John Bevan

Seller of second-hand Catholic books.
www.catholicbooks.co.uk

St Philip's Books

Seller of a range of mainly second-hand books of Catholic interest.
www.stphilipsbooks.co.uk

Catholic Central Library

Based near to Euston Station, with an extensive range of Catholic books
www.catholic-library.org.uk

EXPLORING YOUR FAITH

Catholic Answers

You've got questions? They've got answers.
www.catholic.com

Catholic Apologetics on the Internet

Huge list of responses to potential queries about the Faith
www.cwo.com/~pentrack/catholic/apolo.html

Eucharist

Comprehensive resource on the Eucharist
www.therealpresence.org/eucharst/euch_fr.htm

Evidence for Catholicism from the Bible

An excellent guide to Catholic apologetics
ic.net/~erasmus/RAZHOME.HTM

Faith of JRR Tolkien

If you've enjoyed the Lord of the Rings, then take a look at this
www.ewtn.com/library/homelibr/tolkien.htm

Second Spring

Website of the Chesterton Institute for Faith and Culture, which seeks to evangelise contemporary culture
www.secondspring.co.uk

Theology of the Body

Pope John Paul II's teaching on marriage and sexuality
www.theologyofthebody.net

PRAYER

Daily Mass Readings

www.nccbuscc.org/nab

Holy Rosary

A guide to the recitation of the Rosary
www.newadvent.org/faq/rosary.pdf

Liturgy of the Hours

Texts each day of Morning, Evening and Night Prayer
www.liturgyhours.org

Sacred Space

Be led through a period or prayer in front of your computer
www.jesuit.org.uk/

PRO-LIFE SITES

Feminists for Life

Evidence that authentic feminism is pro-life
www.feministsforlife.org

Human Life International

Worldwide Catholic pro-life organisation
www.hli.org

Priests for Life

A good resource base
www.priestsforlife.org

Pro-life issues

A comprehensive guide to pro-life issues from a Catholic perspective.
ic.net/~erasmus/RAZ207.HTM

ProLife Alliance

Europe's first Pro-Life Political Party
www.prolife.org.uk/

Society for the Protection of Unborn Children

Protecting human life from the moment of conception
www.spuc.org.uk

Women Affirming Life (WAL)

Pro-woman, pro-child, pro-life
www.affirmlife.com

WORLD YOUTH DAYS

World Youth Day 2000 website

www.gmg2000.it/en/index.html

World Youth Day 2005 website

www.wyd2005.org

UNIVERSITY CATHOLIC SOCIETIES

Further details may also be found under the relevant university chaplaincy in the regional listings

Aberdeen University Catholic Society

www.abdn.ac.uk/~src175

University of Bath Catholic Society

www.bath.ac.uk/~su4csoc

University of Bristol Catholic Society

www.ubu.org.uk/main/activities/societies/societieslist/CASSOC

Cardiff University Catholic Society

www.cf.ac.uk/suon/catholic

Durham University Catholic Society

www.durham.ac.uk/cathsoc

University of Exeter Catholic Society

gosh.ex.ac.uk/activities/societies/catholic

University of Glasgow Catholic Society, Turnbull Hall

www.gla.ac.uk/Clubs/Turnbull/turnbull.html

The University of Huddersfield Catholic Society

www.hud.ac.uk/chaplaincy/catholic.html

Hull University Catholic Society

www.hull.ac.uk/cathchap/cathsoc.htm

Imperial College London Catholic Society

union.ic.ac.uk/scc/catholic/index.html

Keele University Catholic Society

www.keele.ac.uk/socs/ks09/index.htm

University of Kent Catholic Society

www.cathsoc.org

Lancaster University Cathsoc

www.lancs.ac.uk/socs/cathsoc

University of Leeds Cathsoc

www.leeds.ac.uk/union/socs/catholic_society

Newcastle-upon-Tyne Catholic Society

www.societies.ncl.ac.uk/cathsoc/home2.html

University of Nottingham Catholic Society

www.nottingham.ac.uk/~oczcath

University of Oxford Catholic Society

users.ox.ac.uk/~cathsoc/indexa.html

Oxford Brookes University Catholic Society

www.brookes.ac.uk/student/union/societies/catholic/society.htm

Plymouth University Catholic Society

www.plymouth-diocese.org.uk/organisations/plym_uni.htm

University of Reading Catholic Society

www.rdg.ac.uk/StUnion/Cath

University of Sheffield Catholic Society

www.shef.ac.uk/~ccf

Sheffield Hallam University

www.shuxi.org.uk

University of Southampton Catholic Society

www.soton.ac.uk/~cathsoc

University of Surrey Catholic Society

www.surrey.ac.uk/Union/societies/CathSoc

The University of York Catholic Student's Society

www-users.york.ac.uk/~socs37

University of Wales, Aberystwyth, Catholic Society

users.aber.ac.uk/scty07

University Of Wales, Swansea, Catholic Society

www.geocities.com/uwscathsoc

University of the West of England

www.uwe.ac.uk/cathsoc

A SELECTION OF RELIGIOUS ORDERS

Augustinians

www.aug.org

Benedictines, Skete

www.sanctiangeli.org

Carmelites

www.ocarm.org/eng/index.htm

Farnborough Abbcy

www.farnboroughabbey.org/homepage.html

Franciscan Friars of the Renewal

www.franciscanfriars.com

Franciscan Sisters of the Renewal

www.franciscansisterscfr.com

Institute of Charity

www.rosmini.org

Montfort Missionaries

homepages.nildram.co.uk/~montfort

Order of Friars Minor

www.friar.org

Order of Preachers (Dominicans)

english.op.org

Redemptorists, Kinnoull

www.kinnoull.org

Poor Clares

www.poorclare.org

St Cecilia's Abbey

www.stceciliasabbey.org.uk

Salesians

www.salesians.org.uk

Society of Jesus (Jesuits)

www.jesuit.co.uk

Stanbrook Abbey

www.stanbrookabbey.org.uk

FURTHER GAP YEAR INFORMATION & OPPORTUNITIES

Action for Children in Conflict
www.actionchildren.org

Action against hunger
www.aahuk.org/home.htm

Association for International Practical Training (AIPT)
Internships and short-term training in the United States
www.aipt.org

BUNAC Working Adventures Worldwide
Offers overseas work/travel programmes offer students and young people.
www.bunac.org.uk

Camp America
Work and travel programmes in the USA
www.campamerica.co.uk

ChildHope UK
Dedicated to improving the lives of street children world-wide
www.childhopeuk.org

Council on International Educational Exchange (CIEE)
Study abroad and work abroad
www.ciee.org

Christians Abroad
www.cabroad.org.uk

Employment advice
www.gapwork.com

Find Your Feet (FYF)
Works in Asia and Africa
www.fyf.org.uk

Health Advice for travellers
www.fco.gov.uk/directory

International Care and Relief
Focuses on the problems faced by children and young people
www.icr.org.uk

Information on gap years
www.gapyear.com

I-to-I UK
Opportunities for volunteer travel and TEFL training.
www.i-to-i.com

OSCAR
The UK-based information service for world mission
www.oscar.org.uk

Raleigh International
Environmental and community projects around the world
www.raleigh.org.uk

Students Partnership Worldwide (SPW)
Works with youth in Africa and Asia, offering teaching opportunities
www.spw.org

Teaching Abroad
Volunteer and work experience placements
www.teaching-abroad.co.uk

Voluntary Service Overseas (VSO)
The international development charity for volunteer professionals
www.vso.org.uk

Volunteering within the UK
www.csv.org.uk

World Challenge expeditions
Offer gap year challenges, focusing on personal development
www.world-challenge.co.uk/html/Home.html

World Vision
Christian development agency
www.wvi.org

World Wide Volunteering
www.worldwidevolunteering.org.uk

Worldwrite
Charity linking young people around the world
www.worldwrite.org.uk/default.htm

OTHER SITES OF INTEREST

INFORM
This organisation operates with the support of both the Home Office and the mainstream Churches. It aims to obtain and make available information about new religious movements or 'cults'.
www.lse.ac.uk/Depts/inform

Visit the companion website to the *Catholic Student Guide*:

www.catholicstudent.net

>>> essential surfing for life at university <<<

Articles:

A home for views on life at university as a Catholic. This area already includes an article on 'Catholic Societies' by Fr Patrick Burke. (Submitted articles will usually be limited to 2,500 words).

Updates to listings:

Find out up-to-date contact information (where available) for entries in the listings of the *Catholic Student Guide*. And do you know of a great organisation that is not included in the listings? Let the editor know!

Links:

All the links in the *Catholic Student Guide*, and more...

Student experiences:

Do you have experience of life at university that you are willing to share with other Catholics? Send it in! (Contributions will usually be limited to 500 words)

Send in your own contribution to the editor c/o the publisher (Family Publications, 6a King Street, Oxford OX2 6DF), or by e-mail: catholicstudent@hotmail.com